All-Star Games

From All-Star Youth Leaders

Group

Loveland, Colorado

Dedication

As this book went to print, Rich Mullins' life on earth and ministry to kids ended. Thanks, Rich, for the music—and the reminder of what God can do with a heart committed to him.

All-Star Games
From All-Star Youth Leaders

Copyright © 1998 Group Publishing, Inc.

Credits
Compiling Author: Mikal Keefer
Editor: Bob Buller
Chief Creative Officer: Joani Schultz
Copy Editor: Julie Meiklejohn
Art Director: Kari K. Monson
Cover Art Director: Jeff A. Storm
Designer: Bill Fisher
Computer Graphic Artist: Joyce Douglas
Cover Designer: Randall Miller
Illustrator: Amy Bryant
Production Manager: Gingar Kunkel

Library of Congress Cataloging-in-Publication Data
All-star games from all-star youth leaders / [compiler, Mikal Keefer].
     p.   cm.
  Includes index.
  ISBN 0-7644-2020-8 (alk. paper)
  1. Group games. 2. Church group work with youth. 3. Group games- -Social aspects. I. Keefer, Mikal, 1954- .
GV1203.A414   1998   97-37805
                                                  CIP

10 9 8 7 6 5 4 3 2 1 07 06 05 04 03 02 01 00 99 98

Printed in the United States of America.

Contents -star youth leaders

Icebreakers and Mixers

Cooperative and Competitive Games

Games That Make a Point

Off-the-Wall Games

Games for Special Days and Events

Introduction

Question: What do these three scenes have in common?

1. A youth group on a retreat in the Rocky Mountains pauses in a meadow. The youth leader gives kids three minutes to see how many plants and insects they can count.

2. Two junior high groups square off for a volleyball game at a Philadelphia YMCA.

3. A youth leader in Hawaii points to a six-foot fence and tells his kids that their job is to get everyone up and over the obstacle—and no one gets lunch until they're all successful.

Answer: Each of these groups is playing a game. You see, contrary to popular opinion, a game is more than a contest to see who comes out ahead. A game is any activity in which one or more people engage for the purpose of fun, amusement, or even learning.

That's why we've included all types of games in *All-Star Games From All-Star Youth Leaders*. In addition to traditional competitive games, you'll find cooperative games that help kids work together, ice-breakers to get kids talking, mixers that nudge kids out of their comfort zones and into new relationships, and games that teach kids profound spiritual truths. You'll also discover off-the-wall games to spice up your regular meetings, games for holidays and other special days, and games to use when you're working with large crowds at special events.

But *All-Star Games From All-Star Youth Leaders* is far more than just a collection of games. This book also contains tips on creating your own games from the ground up and evaluating different kinds of games. You'll discover the tricks that all-star youth workers learned over ten, twenty, or thirty years of ministry—tricks about where to find the best ideas, how to turn a good game into a great game, and what mistakes to avoid—and why.

Along the way you'll learn techniques for predicting which games will grab your kids' attention and which will have them heading for the door. You learn why it's sometimes best to leave a game at home, as well as which games work well in an urban area, a Hispanic church, in Canada, and worldwide.

If you've thought that games are "kids' stuff," you're about to think again. You'll learn why planning the games for your next meeting is just as important as planning what to say during the devotion time.

But before we jump into the actual games, let's lay the groundwork for your ministry's game time by talking about:

★ how to create games that your kids will love,
★ why your games should never create a victim,
★ why culture decides which games will work, and
★ how to evaluate and modify the games that you use.

Ready? Great! Then hold on for a quick education in youth ministry gaming!

How to Create Games That Your Kids Will Love

Fun, like beauty, is in the eye of the beholder. You can spend hours planning a game you're sure your group will love and then watch it bomb. But the same kids might go nuts over slamming soda cans around on a table top.

What gives? How can you know—*in advance*—whether a game will flop or fly? You aren't the only one who wishes you had the secret. Every year, the toy industry bets millions of dollars on how kids will react to games—and the consequences are far more serious than just surviving an awkward meeting.

Consequently, toy companies have invested a fortune developing tools to predict how a game will be received by a target market. Of course, this is great for you because you can use the same tools to make sure that your next game will be met with applause instead of apathy.

Industry insiders say you can't go wrong if you ask the following questions during your planning:

★ Do you know what already works?

Ask yourself what game your teenagers would play if they could play any game they wanted. Better—ask *your kids* which game they would play. It may be that your best new game is a variation of a game your kids already enjoy. Think there's no room for innovation? Stop by a game store and count how many applications there are of "throw the ball."

★ Did you test the game?

Toy companies evaluate potential games the same way you should: they test them. "We go out to schools to let kids play with possible games," says Hasbro Toys spokesperson Linda Baker. "We watch to see how well they like the games. There's no substitute for actually trying games out."

In addition to telling toy companies which games appeal to kids, testing also reveals new possibilities. "There are certain things you expect a kid to do with a toy, and then you see the kids do something entirely different," says former Kenner Toys Product Designer Brent

Eresman. "And that's not bad."

Simply put, *misusing* a toy or game is often more fun than using it according to the instructions. Your youth group could probably offer classic examples of this principle in action. For example, send six junior high boys to the church kitchen with a package of balloons. Ask them to inflate the balloons and then bat them around. What do you think will happen? Chances are, you'll be knee-deep in a water-balloon fight before you can say, "Explain *this* to the church board."

So before you roll out a game for your entire group, test the game with a few kids. Give them the chance to change the rules to make it more fun (though you may have to set limits). When they start using pins you brought for a "decorate the bulletin board" game to perform body piercing on each other—*that's* over the line.

★ Have you planned the game simply and carefully?

Good games take good planning. Design a simple, easily explained game that won't take an engineer to diagram or a professional athlete to play. Issues to consider include the skill levels of your kids, your playing area, safety concerns, and what you're trying to accomplish. Keep in mind that safety hazards are most easily solved during the *planning* stage of your game. Imagine that you're surrounded by parents and lawyers as you plan. Do you really want to dump kids into shopping carts for a speed relay? Probably not. You may not be able to foresee every possible injury, but good planning avoids the vast majority of them.

★ Have you engaged your kids' imagination?

This is easier said than done. "Capturing the imagination is what makes a game fun for older kids," states Eresman. "I'm not sure how you do it. I don't know that there's a foolproof way to say, '*This* will appeal to kids' imaginations.' " Maybe not, but testing games removes those that definitely fall short, and avoiding failure gets you closer to finding success.

★ Are you relying too much on an element of surprise?

Many youth workers introduce surprises into games to keep kids on their toes. They'll change the rules, turn on a sprinkler, or shut off the lights. That's OK, but don't *rely* on surprises to make a game fun. "It's easy to use the element of surprise with small children," says Eresman, "but with teenagers, it's tough." The problem is that too many surprises lead kids to look for more. They anticipate your next move. A better strategy is to design games that don't require a surprise to be fun.

★ Does the game help teenagers meet others?

You're dealing with a relational crowd. Any game that helps kids meet others has an advantage over games that isolate them. One toy-industry representative explains: "There's a reason there aren't a lot of games put out for older children. For teenagers, relationships are paramount. Put out a game that helps kids hang out with friends and meet members of the opposite sex, and you'll have a very successful game."

Note this key secret of successful gaming: Consider how the game makes your kids look to others. Teenagers are hungry for popularity, self-esteem, relationships, and respect from others. So they won't take kindly to games that leave them looking like village idiots. Games that set kids up to look foolish in front of others often lead to long-term problems—which brings us to our next point.

Why Your Games Should Never Create a Victim

"Never make the crowd, someone else, or yourself into a victim," states Group Publishing founder Thom Schultz. "Crowdbreakers and stunts that demean someone may do damage in ways you can't see." Schultz shakes his head sadly as he relates: "I did some things as a young youth worker that I still regret. I was in youth ministry with the same kids long enough to hear them reflect back on some games and say, 'I never got over that. It really bothered me.'

"Let's not teach kids to victimize people. It doesn't matter *who* the victim is. It doesn't matter if the victim is *willing*. What we're teaching is that it's OK to laugh at a victim. We don't need activities and games that teach kids to laugh at the unfortunate."

Often, kids who are subjected to ridicule don't get indignant and stalk out. They're expected to be "good sports," so they laugh along with the joke (played at their expense), slide back into their seats, and carry on as if nothing happened.

But don't count on those kids coming back. One youth worker recalls an incident from early in his career. "We picked a kid to do a goofy thing," he reports, "and it absolutely didn't work." The game involved seating a girl in a chair facing the audience. Behind her, another teenager was blindfolded and handed a tube of lipstick and a hairbrush. The blindfolded teenager was to put the lipstick on the girl's face and then comb her hair.

"She ended up with lipstick all over her face," recalls the youth worker, "and was terribly embarrassed. If this girl had known what was going to happen, it may have been all right. But in her eyes, she was made fun of rather than having fun—she never came back."

Don't let one person's embarrassment be the reason that others are laughing. Just because the victim is laughing doesn't mean that he or she is having fun. Before you play any game, ask yourself the following questions:

1. Does it single out one or more kids for any kind of ridicule or embarrassment?

2. Is there any chance that you might have to say, "Come on, be a good sport"?

If you answer "yes" to either question, scratch the game. Finally, before you add any game to your meeting, ask if there's any reason it might not fit your group. Some games—even the proven games in this book—may not work with your group or your setting. Your group has a unique culture, and ignoring it is a guaranteed ticket to disaster. In fact, knowing your group's "culture" is so crucial that we've devoted an entire section to it.

Why Culture Decides Which Games Will Work

Most game books seem to come with several built-in assumptions: that you are a youth leader in America, that your group is primarily white, and that your group is essentially middle-class and suburban.

But if your group doesn't resemble this stereotype or you intend to lead games in another culture—on a short-term mission trip, for example—you'll benefit from considering how culture affects games. Here's what youth workers who have been there have learned.

★ Play by their rules.

Crossing social lines and stepping on a cultural land mine will not only bring whatever game you're playing to a screeching halt, it may irreparably damage your credibility. For instance, a man touching a woman outside of marriage—however innocently—is taboo in the Thai and Arab cultures. If you were to organize a game for teenagers from these cultures, it would be wise to divide teams into guys' and girls' groups if there's any touching involved.

John Sanny, who has organized and led thousands of games with groups throughout the Pacific Rim for Youth With A Mission, says the smart thing to do is not to introduce American games at all. "Find out what games they play and join in," says Sanny. "Then, when they feel good about you in their culture, you can introduce some of your games."

Of course, this means that if the local game of choice is balancing coconuts or another game you've never played, you're going to lose— a lot. And that's not all bad. "Let the local kids show you the ropes and be the experts," advises Sanny. "You'll build relationships far faster than if you attempt to convince kids to play an unfamiliar game only you can win."

And when the time comes for you to introduce a game, don't start with Monopoly. Games that require lots of explanation or involve too many details aren't going to work. "Games need to be spontaneous, relational things that don't take a lot of thinking," explains Sanny. "You can't stand there and explain a game—in a foreign culture or in your own culture. Rather, give kids a step-by-step demonstration. If you tell them the whole thing up front, they get spooked. Start by telling them, 'OK, everyone on the floor.' Then take them to the next step. The surprise comes at the end when they're actually *playing* the game." Finally, go easy on competitive games, cautions Sanny. "Use easy, relational games that don't create divisions. Competition is a Western thing."

★ **Respect their sensibilities.**

Cultural differences aren't a concern only when you cross an ocean. Mary Arias, a youth worker in southern California, suggests that wacky games and the Hispanic community aren't necessarily a comfortable fit. "In the Hispanic community, church is *church,* and you don't normally play games in church. So I have to plan a special event—a party or an overnighter—in order to have games."

It's not just disapproving adults who frown on games. "Kids who retain a lot of their Hispanic culture are stricter themselves," says Arias. "They don't wear pants or shorts to church, which makes it hard to play some games." Arias has discovered that, for games to work with her kids, the games must be totally inoffensive. "These kids don't want to play a lot of touching games—or games with any kind of sexual connotation."

Expense is another consideration when she decides which games to use. "Accessibility to materials is an issue in poorer churches," she explains. Games that require expensive supplies or that waste materials are simply not an option. Finally, Arias looks for games that connect the members of her group. "If kids can encourage each other while they play a game, their walls start to come down—and that's fantastic."

In Toronto, on the other hand, Miranda Farrell-Myers laments that her group won't try anything that involves the possibility of "getting germs." "Hygiene is an issue here," she says. "My kids don't want to deal with food or play any game that would muss up their hair. They won't sit on the floor—it would mess up their clothes. Don't even try a game that involves everyone taking off his or her shoes and trying on other kids' shoes—it simply won't work." So if appearance is very important to your kids, design games with that concern in mind. Ask yourself: What *else* is a part of their unique culture?

★ Understand their culture.

Culture varies even within a geographical area, so you must take *your* group's culture into account. For example, urban and suburban cultures simply aren't identical. As director of the Fellowship of Christian Athletes in Washington, D.C., Steve Fitzhugh works with teenagers in an urban setting. Playing games is about the furthest thing from his kids' minds.

"This particular generation is really grown up," he observes. "I deal with seventeen-year-old kids who are heads of their houses, who have children. I find ways to *force* kids to play. I'm very intentional about getting them involved, to give them time just to be kids."

It's not an easy task for Fitzhugh, who designs group-involvement games and competitive situations so kids find it difficult to opt out of participating. Fitzhugh believes that the benefits make the effort worthwhile. "Kids start to laugh, and it's *good* for them," he says.

Bart Campolo, founder and president of Kingdom Builders Supply, finds that *not* forcing urban kids to participate in games works best. "When I began as a youth worker, we had a fixation on 'everyone has to play,' " explains Campolo. But working with urban kids has forced Campolo to reconsider. "I've seen fistfights. I've seen youth workers get cold-cocked because they were in someone's face saying, 'Come on! You *gotta* play!' "

Campolo doesn't pressure kids to get involved. Rather, he tries to "organize an alternative for kids who don't want to play. You really need to have something prepared," he says.

So how important is it that your kids join in games? It depends. If your kids' culture is best served by requiring participation—do it. If, on the other hand, their culture might react negatively to compelled participation, find some other creative alternative to participation in the game.

In sum, to work, games must be *fun*—and what constitutes "fun" varies from group to group and from culture to culture. It makes sense, then, to take advantage of whatever "safe" games already exist in a group's culture. "It comes down to an issue of respect," explains a veteran missionary who has worked in various cultures. "You earn it. If you start by listening, learning, and sharing in your host culture's games, you'll get a lot further than by imposing American culture on them. People may politely let you win the battle—but you've lost the war."

How to Evaluate and Modify the Games That You Use

Games are like every other part of your program: You want to be sure that they work. And if your only yardstick for success is how many kids applauded, you may be missing the mark. If you played a particular game for a particular reason, it's worth evaluating the results. One way to evaluate games is by asking a few questions.

★ **Did most kids participate in some way?**

If a number of kids refused to play or played halfheartedly, your game is probably on life support. But before you pull the plug, make sure the problem wasn't just bad timing or your poor explanation of the game. Even if kids *didn't* participate, the game might still be a success if you discover why they didn't participate and do something to fix it.

★ **Did the game accomplish the goals you set for it?**

If you were playing the game just for fun, did kids have fun? If you were trying to promote cooperation, did kids cooperate? If you were trying to teach a lesson, did kids learn it? Never play a game without knowing why you are playing it or without asking yourself how well the game achieved your goals.

In addition, always debrief learning games. It's the only way to know if kids learned the lesson you wanted. "Debriefing" is simply discussing the game experience and helping kids identify what they felt and learned during the game. It usually works best if you form pairs, trios, or small groups of kids for discussion so everyone can participate. Finally, keep the discussion going by asking open-ended questions that invite kids to share in their groups. Debriefing helps kids get involved and thinking. It also enables you to find out if they learned the lesson of the game.

★ **What does your Game Review Committee think?**

You *do* have a Game Review Committee, don't you? A Game Review Committee is a small, handpicked group of kids who tell you what they think of the games you play. Make sure that your committee includes a representative from each part of your group—younger, older, male, and female. Ask kids to tell you what went well and what didn't—so you can improve your chances of delivering quality programming.

Ask your committee questions such as "What was best about this game?" "What was worst about it?" "How did you feel as you played the game?" "What did the game communicate?" and "Would you want a friend to play this game? Why or why not?"

★ **Did the game communicate anything you didn't want to communicate?**

If for any reason you suspect that a game damaged someone's self-esteem or left kids misunderstanding the point of the game, ask your group about it. Go to the person who may not have enjoyed the experience, and find out what happened. Ask your kids what they think the game was teaching and then help them discover what it was meant to teach. If a game sent a wrong message, go back and repair the damage at once.

Once you've evaluated a game, you're ready to change it however you want and need. Don't think of these (or any other) games as set in stone. Rules are given because they work in most cases. The rules have been field-tested with other groups, but they are not the only way these games will work. Sometimes you can turn a competitive game into a cooperative game in which everyone "competes" to achieve a task. (See Chapter 2 for specific examples.) Maybe you can adapt a just-for-fun game into a learning experience that teaches kids a crucial biblical truth. (See Chapter 3 to discover how this works.) However you do it, make sure that you adapt the games in this book or any other games that you use so they fit your group's culture *and* accomplish your game goals.

Youth group games are like folk songs—they change as they move from group to group. Someone adds a twist here or modifies a rule there, and the game changes as it passes through different groups' hands. And that's exactly as it should be. Modify these games to fit your group and your situation. *All-Star Games From All-Star Youth Leaders* isn't the Official and Final Rule Book for these time-tested games. Use these games, but make them yours as you adapt and alter them to help your kids enjoy a good time, grow closer together, and learn more about God and his wonderful plan for their lives.

Icebreakers and Mixers

What do you do when you have a room full of kids who don't know each other well (or at all) and it's your job to get them talking with each other and learning together?

You involve kids in an icebreaker or a mixer! Icebreakers get kids talking by comfortably leading them through the awkward first few minutes of any relationship. Mixers, on the other hand, move kids around, shifting them out of their "comfort-zone groups" (commonly called cliques) so they learn more about those they generally tend to avoid.

One word of caution, however. Both ice-breakers and mixers tinker with teenagers' social lives, so it's important that you respect kids' sensibilities. Kids, like most adults, are especially vulnerable when they're new to the group or surrounded by people they don't know all that well. So it's absolutely essential that icebreakers and mixers be as nonthreatening as possible and that nobody feels singled out or embarrassed. The goal is to help kids feel comfortable with each other, so avoid doing anything that might make the kids in your group feel ill at ease.

For example, it's surprisingly easy to offend kids when you ask them to gather in small groups. You could ask kids to form groups of eight and then line up according to height. It sounds innocent enough, but how will the five-foot-ten-inch junior high girl or the four-foot-eleven-inch senior high boy feel about it? Having one's height (or lack thereof) highlighted in a lineup can be embarrassing.

What if you have kids line up by foot length? Same problem. You need to remember that most kids are exceptionally self-conscious about their bodies and don't want undue attention drawn to them.

A better approach is to group kids according to traits other than physical attributes. (This can also help kids learn more about each other.) For example, you might have kids line up in the order of their birthdays or according to how close to your meeting room they were born. You could also have them form groups of those who

★ were born during the same season,

★ are wearing the same color socks,

15

★ are wearing similar kinds of shoes,
★ listen to the same kind of music,
★ like the same television show, or
★ have owned the same pet (or no pet).

The possibilities are endless, so use your imagination to group and mix your kids for maximum relationship-building results.

Icebreakers and mixers, like all tools, are only as effective as the person using them. Used properly, they can break down the walls that separate kids and lay the foundation for healthy relationships within the group. Used improperly, they can damage kids or even drive them away from the group. Remember: Kids are especially vulnerable when they are surrounded by peers they don't know well.

So use the icebreakers and mixers that follow to help your kids feel comfortable as they talk with one another and get to know each other a little better than they did before.

Affirmation Bingo icebreakers and mixers
Wayne Rice

Game Summary: Kids will give—and receive—affirmations in a game of Bingo in which everyone's a winner.

Game Supplies: You'll need photocopies of the "Affirmation Bingo" handout (p. 31) and pencils.

The Game:
Before the meeting, make one copy of the "Affirmation Bingo" handout for each person. When you're ready to play the game, give everyone a copy of the handout and a pencil.

Explain that this game is like regular Bingo except that kids fill squares by affirming others in the ways described. Whenever someone completes the action on a square, the affirmed person should write his or her name across the appropriate square on the other person's card. Kids may not get the same person's signature twice until they have five squares completed in a row, which is a Bingo.

Challenge kids to see how many Bingos they can complete in five minutes. When time is up, signal the end of the game and ask kids to report how many Bingos they have completed and squares they have filled.

If group members are just learning each other's names, have each group member read the name of each person who signed his or her card and point to the person whose name is being read.

e x t e n s i o n idea

Increase the significance of this game by having kids form small groups to discuss the following questions:

★ What did you like about affirming others? being affirmed?

★ What was difficult about affirming others? What was easy?

★ What can we do to genuinely affirm each other all the time?

Coats of Arms icebreakers and mixers
Michael D. Warden

Game Summary: Kids will create distinctive—and personalized—shields that tell something about themselves.

Game Supplies: You'll need newsprint, colored markers (or crayons), and tape or tacks.

The Game:

Before the meeting, draw an outline of a coat of arms on a sheet of newsprint (see diagram) and hang it where everyone can see it.

To begin, form groups of three to five. Give each group a sheet of newsprint and several markers. Explain that families in medieval Europe often designed coats of arms that used images and symbols to describe the chief characteristics of the family. For example, a coat of arms might use a bee to signify that the family is hard-working or a lion to represent the family's strength.

If no one has any questions about coats of arms, instruct groups to draw an outline of a coat of arms on their newsprint. Then have each member of the group add a symbol that describes something about him or her. The symbol can be a drawing of an actual object, such as an animal or a plant, or some other kind of representative shape, such as a

tion idea

to fit the
n by having
s that
feel about
tha   example, if you're
teaching about kids' relationships with God, you may ask
them to design symbols that
represent how they feel about
God. This could prompt everything from a flame to a "Do Not
Disturb" sign.

heart or possibly a square.

Allow groups five to ten minutes to work and then ask kids to share in their groups what their symbols mean. After five minutes, have each group join another group. Then have kids in each group take turns explaining the meanings of other group members' symbols to the larger group. To help kids learn more about each other, have each original group join yet another group and repeat the process. This time, however, have each person tell about a different group member's symbol. Continue until each person has heard about everyone else's symbol.

⭐Common Ground icebreakers and mixers
Wayne Rice

Game Summary: Teams will race to create lists of things that all the team members have in common.

Game Supplies: You'll need paper and pencils.

The Game:
Form equal-sized teams of three to six. Give each team a sheet of paper and a pencil. Tell teams their challenge is to list everything they can think of that all team members have in common. For example, team members might all attend the same school, prefer the same kind of music, or like the same brand of tennis shoes. The only rule is that they can't list similar body parts, such as "We all have two arms, a brain, and a nose."

⭐ **All-Star** ⭐
advice

According to Wayne, "Kids really have to work hard after they list about a dozen things they have in common. But the payoff is worth the effort."

Tell teams they have three minutes to create their lists, so they need to work quickly. (Groups of five or six may need more time, but don't allow more than four to five minutes.) To add to the urgency and excitement of the game, inform teams when there is one minute as well as thirty seconds remaining.

When time is up, find out which team has the longest list and ask team members to read the similarities they listed. Then ask teams who had similarities not already listed to share them. To conclude, have the entire group discuss the following questions. Ask:

★ **How easy was it to discover something in common with another team member? with every team member?**

★ **What does this reveal about the extent to which we're alike? the ways in which we're all different?**

★ **How can our similarities draw us closer together? How can our differences help us grow closer?**

Variation idea

Challenge teams to list things members don't have in common—things that make each person unique. For example, kids may have been born in different states, might go to different schools, or might have different favorite music groups. You might also challenge your entire youth group to list as many things as it can that members all have in common.

Human Knot icebreakers and mixers
Thom Schultz

Game Summary: Kids will hold hands in a convoluted grouping and then work to untangle themselves without letting go of each other's hands.

Game Supplies: No supplies are required.

The Game:

Have kids stand in a tight circle. (If you have more than ten kids in your group, have kids form multiple groups of ten or fewer.) Ask kids to stretch their right hands into the circle and grab anyone else's hand except that of the person standing next to them. Then have kids repeat the process with their left hands, making sure not to hold both hands of the same person.

Once kids are linked, explain that they must untangle themselves without letting go of each other's hands. They can step over, crawl under, or slide between each other to get untangled. Kids may even readjust their grips to avoid

★ *All-Star* ★ advice

Take extra care when games require kids to touch each other. These kinds of games can be wonderful relationship-builders, but they can also lead to embarrassing situations. Be careful when you use games that highlight kids' bodies or require kids to engage in close contact. Teenagers are remarkably sensitive, so if there's a chance someone may be emotionally hurt—don't use the game.

twisting anyone's arm, but they must not let go of the hands they're holding!

After kids have untangled themselves, ask the entire group the following questions:

★ **What was an effective strategy for untangling the knot?**
★ **How important was cooperation in untangling this knot?**
★ **What are some knots in your life that you're untangling?**
★ **How might you work with others to untangle those knots?**

Name Game icebreakers and mixers
John Sanny

Game Summary: Kids will be challenged to remember each other's names as quickly as they can.

Game Supplies: You'll need a king-size bedsheet or a tarp.

The Game:

Ask kids to stand in a circle. Then direct kids to go around the circle introducing themselves by first name. Repeat the process several times so kids become familiar with each other's names.

Then have kids form two teams. (If you have more than twenty-four kids in your group, you may want to have kids form four teams of twelve or fewer and play two games at the same time.)

Have two adult leaders (or one volunteer from each team) hold up the bedsheet to form a barrier. Direct teams to line up on opposite sides of the bedsheet, making sure teams can't see each other. Explain that each team is to silently choose one member to stand about six inches from the bedsheet, facing it.

When both kids are in position, the adult leaders will drop the bedsheet and kids are each to attempt to say the opposing player's name first—without the help of teammates. Whoever comes in second is out of the game. If neither person can name the other team's player, both are eliminated. Continue until one team has no members left.

Variation idea

If your kids already know each other's names fairly well, use this activity to help kids learn something new about each other. Choose a detail to have kids share about their lives, such as their favorite toy as a preschooler or the month of their birth. Make sure the answers are only one word long, so when the bedsheet falls both players have short answers to shout out.

On-Site Scavenger Hunt icebreakers and mixers
Joani Schultz

Game Summary: Kids will use their imaginations to find scavenger hunt items within the room.
Game Supplies: You'll need masking tape.

The Game:
Have kids form two teams. If you have more than twenty kids in your group, have kids form multiple teams of ten or fewer. Place a masking tape X in the center of the room. (If you have four or more teams, make one X for every two teams. Keep the Xs several feet apart.)

Tell kids that they're about to go on a scavenger hunt inside the meeting room. You'll read a description of an object and then teams are to figure out what object in the room matches that description. As soon as a team finds the object, it is to send a representative to stand on the X. (If you are using multiple Xs, continue playing until all the Xs are covered.)

If you decide that a team's object matches the description, you will award that team 100 points and start a new round. If an object doesn't match the description, teams will continue looking.

Answer any questions and then read the following clues (but not the suggested answers, which are in parentheses) one at a time:

★ A face without any eyes (a watch)

★ Pictures of three political leaders (on coins and currency)

★ A source of illumination (a flashlight, a match, or an illuminated watch-face)

★ A script for the movie *The Ten Commandments* (a Bible)

★ Two black eyes (sunglasses)

★ A star (any star shape or a picture of a movie star)

★ A picture of the White House (the back of an American twenty-dollar bill)

★ A picture of "the lamp of the body" (any picture that depicts someone's eyes)

Variation idea

If you want to play this game again but don't want to think up new clues, have your group members create them. Give each team two sheets of paper and a pencil. Have each team list ten objects and clues describing those objects on one sheet of paper. Then have each team write the ten clues (but not the objects) on the second sheet of paper. Collect both sets of papers and then distribute clue sheets to teams, making sure no team gets its own clues. Have teams race to find all the objects on their lists. Use the sheets of paper with objects and clues on them to check that teams have found the proper objects.

★ The key to thousands of books (a library card)

★ A set of colored teeth (a comb)

★ The official seal of your state or province (check your driver's license)

Total teams' points and then award a round of applause first to the winning team and then to everyone for a creative game well played!

One-Minute Missionaries

icebreakers and mixers

Michael D. Warden

Game Summary: Kids will be commissioned to do tremendously good deeds that take sixty seconds or less.

Game Supplies: No supplies are required.

The Game:

Have kids form trios. Ask trio members to decide which one will be a Stop Sign, which will be a Yield Sign, and which will be a No-Passing Sign. Tell kids that the Stop Signs will begin this game as Commanders and that Yield Signs and No-Passing Signs will act as Agents. Everyone will have a turn to be a Commander.

Explain that this game is called One-Minute Missionaries and that kids will compete to show kindness to each other. Commanders will tell their Agents to do something affirming for someone in the room, and Agents have to do it. There are only two guidelines:

★ Commanders can only tell their Agents to do or say things that are honestly affirming and encouraging to others, and

★ When Agents finish their missions, they are to return to their Commanders and say, "Mission accomplished."

Allow Commanders a minute to think up their encouraging missions. For example, a Commander might say: "See that guy in the yellow shirt? Go tell him he's the best-looking, kindest-hearted guy I know." Another Commander might send an Agent to give a particular girl a friendly hug. Remind

> ### ★ All-Star advice ★
>
> Kids enjoy being complimented and affirmed, but beware of robbing affirmations of their meaning by forcing or coercing them. Encourage kids to affirm each other often, but insist that they always do so genuinely and honestly. Spontaneous and genuine recognitions of one's strengths and accomplishments mean much more than forced and contrived compliments.

Commanders that the missions can be verbal (things to say), nonverbal (things to do), or combinations of the two—but the missions must be honest and affirming. (If any Agent is told to do something that makes him or her extremely uncomfortable, the Agent may tell the Commander "Mission impossible" and the Commander must give the Agent a new mission.)

When all the Commanders have decided on missions, tell Agents that they have one minute to carry out their missions. If Agents return before the minute is up, Commanders may give them another assignment.

After one minute, call time and announce that the Yield Signs are now the Commanders. Have these new Commanders decide on missions and send out their Agents. Repeat the process with the No-Passing Signs as Commanders.

After everyone has acted as a Commander, ask for volunteers to report how they were affirmed and encouraged. Then ask the entire group the following questions:

★ **Did you prefer being sent out or sending others out? Why?**
★ **How did you feel about having others sent to affirm you?**
★ **How can we genuinely encourage each other all the time?**

Pass the Beans icebreakers and mixers
Joani Schultz

Game Summary: Kids will try to collect beans by listing their unique experiences and talents.

Game Supplies: You'll need fifteen beans for each person.

The Game:

The goal of this game is for kids to learn about each other and to discover that each person has unique experiences and talents to bring to the group.

Challenge kids to line up in order of their birthdays as fast as they can. Then form groups of five, with the first five kids in line making up one group, the next five another group, and so on.

Ask members of each group to sit in a circle. Give each person fifteen beans. Explain that group members are to try to collect beans by describing their unique experiences or abilities. For example, a person might tell about running in a 15K race, winning a coloring contest when he or she was four, being able to wiggle his or her ears, or being able to recite the books of the Bible backward. Remind kids that every activity they describe must be absolutely true.

After someone shares a unique activity or ability, each group member who hasn't done that activity or doesn't have that ability must give that person one bean. Have group members take turns listing their unique experiences and abilities until each person has shared ten activities.

After everyone in each group has listed ten activities, ask kids to report how many beans they've collected. Then ask for volunteers to report to the entire group interesting activities they heard about. Encourage kids who have done an activity being reported to tell about their experiences.

Allow several minutes for groups to report and then challenge group members to take turns listing experiences and abilities they think everyone in the group has done or has. This time, however, the person naming an activity must give a bean to anyone who has not done the activity. Encourage kids to describe specific and creative activities, avoiding common activities such as getting out of bed, going to the store, or being able to breathe.

After everyone has listed ten activities, ask kids to report how many beans they have. Encourage kids to give themselves a round of applause. Then close with a reminder that each person present is a unique and valued member of the group and that they all can share in the joy of learning about God together.

e x t e n s i o n idea

To get kids thinking about the significance of this game, ask them to discuss the following questions in their small groups:

★ How easy was it to list things no one else has done? activities everyone has done?

★ What does this reveal about ways we are all alike? ways each person is unique?

★ If you could do one of the activities you heard described, which would it be? Why?

★ How can our unique experiences make our group stronger? How can our shared experiences make our group stronger?

Penny Pinch icebreakers and mixers
Thom Schultz

Game Summary: Kids will compete to collect and then give away pennies.
Game Supplies: You'll need ten pennies for each group member.

The Game:

Give each person ten pennies. Explain that kids have two minutes to collect as many pennies as they can from each other. The rules for collecting pennies are as follows:

★ Kids are to collect pennies by asking others for them; they may not forcibly take pennies from others.

★ Anyone asked for a penny must hand it over *unless* he or she has the same color eyes as the person asking.

★ A person may not request a penny from the same person twice until he or she has asked everyone else in the group.

If everyone understands the rules, start the game. To add to the chaos, play loud music and periodically announce how much time is remaining. Cut the music off abruptly at the end of two minutes, and ask kids to count their pennies to discover who has the most. Then announce that there is a second round to play.

Explain that this time kids will have three minutes to give away as many pennies as possible. The rules for giving away pennies are as follows:

★ A person may not give away a penny until he or she gives the person being given the penny an honest and specific compliment.

★ A person may give only one penny and one compliment to each person until he or she has complimented everyone in the group.

Allow kids a minute to think of specific and honest compliments. Suggest that kids offer compliments such as "I enjoy your friendly smile" or "That's a beautiful sweater that you're wearing." After a minute, begin the game and play soft music (so as to not drown out conversations). Keep kids posted on time remaining. When time is up, ask kids to count their

Variation idea

If kids don't know each other's names well, use the following idea in place of the first round. Tell kids that the person being asked for a penny must give it to the person asking, if his or her first name shares a letter with the first name of the person asking. For example, if Mike asked Tiffany for a penny, Tiffany would give him one because their names both contain the letter "i." If however, Mike asked Susan for a penny, she would not give him a penny because their names don't share any letters in common. You might also want to play another round using kids' last names.

pennies to discover who has the fewest pennies. Then have kids form small groups to discuss the following questions. Ask:

★ **What did you like about collecting pennies? giving them away?**

★ **Which of the two rounds did you like most? Why did you like it?**

★ **Which compliment was the most enjoyable to give? to receive?**

Personal Parables icebreakers and mixers
Karen Dockrey

Game Summary: Kids will use objects found in the room or in their possession to tell stories about themselves.

Game Supplies: No supplies are required.

The Game:

Ask kids to form groups of five or six based on whether they're "pack rats" or "throw-it-out types." Then instruct group members to introduce themselves to each other (if needed) and to tell one thing they own that they would never throw out.

After several minutes of discussion, explain that Jesus taught profound spiritual truths by telling stories about everyday objects—by telling parables. For example, Jesus compared God's kingdom to a mustard seed to explain how something that begins small can grow to a great size.

Tell kids you'd like them to do the same thing by choosing and using objects from the room, their purses, or their pockets to tell their group members an important thing about themselves. For example, someone might choose a driver's license and explain that she delivers pizzas. Someone else could use a library card to represent his desire to be a novelist. Encourage listeners to ask questions to learn as much about the speakers as they can.

After kids tell their parables, ask each person to tell the entire

Variation idea

Modify this activity to fit the topic of your lesson. For example, if the lesson is on family relationships, have kids use objects to tell about their families. If the lesson is on music, have kids use objects to represent their favorite songs or performers.

group about the person to his or her left by summarizing that person's parable.

Roving Bingo icebreakers and mixers
Thom Schultz

Game Summary: Kids will play Bingo to discover interesting facts about each other.

Game Supplies: You'll need a pair of scissors, pencils, and photocopies of the "Roving Bingo" handout (pp. 32-33).

The Game:

Before the meeting, photocopy and cut apart the sections of the "Roving Bingo" handout (pp. 32-33). You'll need one section for each group member. You can give each person a copy of the same section, distribute several different sections among your group members, or play four rounds, using a different section for each round.

To begin, give everyone a pencil and a section from the "Roving Bingo" handout. Tell kids that they are to find others who can sign their names to and answer the questions for each square. Each person may not have the same person sign his or her card twice, and kids have only four minutes to finish, so they need to work quickly.

Answer any questions and then begin the game. You may want to play soft background music while kids are working. Provide two-minute-, one-minute-, and thirty-second warnings.

After four minutes, call time. Ask kids how many squares they got signed. (If you're going to play another round, encourage kids to try to get new people to sign the squares on their cards.) Then ask kids to share some of the things they discovered about each other.

All-Star advice

"Kids want relationships, to feel as though they're entering into something with you. The youth director's job is not only to show enthusiasm but also to watch for kids who are being marginalized and to draw them into the center of what's going on. An activity is an excuse to get involved with kids."—
Rich Mullins

If group members are just getting to know each other, conclude the game by having kids form small groups to discuss the following questions:

★ How did you feel about asking questions of people you didn't know well?

★ How did you feel about telling strangers personal details about your life?

★ How is this game similar to the way we make friends? How is it different?

Same Game icebreakers and mixers
Karen Dockrey

Game Summary: Kids will identify similarities to uncover connections they already have but may not have been aware of.

Game Supplies: You'll need newsprint, tape, a marker, index cards, and pencils.

The Game:

Before the meeting, write the following sentence across the top of a sheet of newsprint: " ____ and I are similar because we…" Then list the following sample similarities below the sentence:

★ have the same home state.
★ laugh the same way.
★ like the same movie star.
★ have the same favorite song.
★ like the same pizza toppings.
★ have the same eye color.
★ wear the same style of shoes.
★ have the same number of siblings.
★ have the same middle initial.
★ like the same subject at school.
★ have the same after-school job.
★ like the same kind of sandwich.

Finally, hang the newsprint where everyone will be able to see it.

Give each person an index card and a pencil. Then say: **Form a pair with someone you don't know well and write on your card that person's first name and five things the two of you share in common. I've listed sample similarities on this poster, but don't limit yourself to these.**

Allow kids five minutes to complete their lists. Then instruct kids to find other partners they do not know well and repeat the process on the backs of their cards.

After another five minutes, ask each person to introduce both of his or her partners by name and to list his or her similarities with each partner. This will enable the group to discover ten things about each person.

After everyone has introduced his or her partners, ask the entire group the following questions:

★ **Why is it important for us to share similarities with others? to be unique in some ways?**

★ **How can we use our similarities to grow closer as a group? How can we use our differences?**

Conclude by encouraging kids to develop or deepen relationships within the group by taking time to discover both their similarities and their unique characteristics.

extension idea

After each person lists five similarities with his or her first partner, have pairs join to form foursomes. Then have kids list at least five similarities that all four group members share. Continue combining small groups until the entire group lists everything that all the members share in common.

Speed Ball icebreakers and mixers
Joanne Knittle

Game Summary: Kids will learn each other's names as they quickly pass a foam ball around a circle.

Game Supplies: You'll need a foam ball.

The Game:

Ask kids to form a standing circle. Give a foam ball to the person wearing the most yellow. Instruct that person to call out his or her first name and then toss the ball across the circle to someone else. That person should then call out his or her name and toss the ball to someone else. Have kids continue the process until the ball has been tossed to everyone. (Kids can either toss the ball randomly around the circle or toss it in a set pattern. The latter will ensure that no one is left out.)

Encourage kids to keep the ball moving as fast as they can. After several minutes, tell kids that, instead of saying their own names, they now must each call out the name of the person they'll be tossing the ball to.

Challenge kids to see how long they can play without forgetting someone's name. When kids have learned each other's names (or if your group members know each other fairly well), have kids call out their favorite colors, favorite television shows, the names of their first pets, the third digits in their phone numbers, or the colors of the walls in their rooms.

Affirmation Bingo handout

Thank someone for something specific.	Give someone a shoulder rub.	Compliment some- one's favorite food.	Tell someone what he or she adds to the group.	Hum someone's favorite song.
Compliment someone else's hairstyle.	Say "I'm glad you're here!" and mean it.	List three good things about someone.	Smile at someone for thirty seconds.	Say a prayer of blessing for someone.
Recite a few lines of a nice poem or song.	Share something you have with you.	Tell someone you care about him or her.	Bow and tell some- one he or she is wonderful.	Compliment someone else's shoes or clothes.
Give someone a friendly hug.	Laugh at someone's favorite joke.	Say, "God and I love you!" to someone.	Applaud someone who hums to you.	Offer someone a chair to sit in.
Ask "How are you?" and listen to the answer.	Share an encourag- ing thought or story.	Compliment some- one's taste in music.	Offer someone something to drink.	State a positive wish for someone.

Roving Bingo handout

Around the House

_____ owns a water cannon. Who has been soaked? Who would you like to soak?	_____ owns an umbrella. What color is it? Where did you get it?
_____ drinks at least two glasses of water a day. How many glasses do you drink total? What's your favorite soft drink?	_____ likes to stay up late. What's your favorite late-night activity? What's your favorite late-night snack?

Beach Bums

_____ has put sunscreen on his or her nose. When did you use sunscreen? Why did you use sunscreen?	_____ has found a sand dollar on the beach. Where was it found? When was it found?
_____ has swum in the Pacific Ocean. When were you there? Why were you there?	_____ wears a swimming cap. What color is it? Why do you wear it?

Roving Bingo handout

Sports Fanatics

_____ has scored a goal in soccer. When did you play? How many goals did you score?	_____ has made a three-point shot in basketball. When did you first do it? How many three-point shots have you made?
_____ can water- or snow-ski. When did you learn to ski? Where do you like to ski?	_____ has hit a home run. What position did you play? How many home runs have you hit?

School Daze

_____ has been home schooled. When were you home schooled? What did you like most about it?	_____ has gone to at least five schools. Which schools did you attend? Which school was best? worst?
_____ knows last year's locker combination. What is the combination? What's in your current locker?	_____ has been in the teachers' lounge. When were you in there? What was it like?

Competitive and Cooperative Games

Competition. Think of it as a fire that suddenly appears outside your youth room. Bring it in, and you may find a wonderful source of heat, light, and an occasional lesson illustration. But then again, it just might burn down your church building, too!

A Brief History of Competition and Cooperation

Youth ministry in the 1960s was *packed* with competition. Kids competed against each other in everything from balloon volleyball to Bible memorization. There were winners, there were losers, and it didn't take long to figure out who was who.

Sometime in the 1970s, however, the pendulum swung toward a kinder, gentler youth ministry. Youth leaders developed cooperative games that deliberately included everyone, made sure everyone could (or would) win, and gave everyone the experience of succeeding.

Since then the pendulum has swung again, this time back toward the middle, as some youth workers have tried to include both types of games. "At one time we were afraid to do anything competitive," explains Jim Burns. "Then Willow Creek and several other programs reintroduced competition—but with two important features. First, competition must be *team*-based, with points awarded for winning a relay or for bringing a visitor. Second, games should give everyone a realistic chance to win."

In spite of this latest trend, some youth workers remain hesitant to use competitive games. If you find yourself in this category, read on!

The Pros and Cons of Competition

Whatever youth workers think of competition, they all agree on one point: It permeates a teenager's life. "Before kids ever come to the meeting, they've already endured a full day of competition at school," observes Susie Shellenberger. "Whether it's for grades, friends, the opposite sex's attention, or a spot on the cheerleading squad, kids are used to competition."

In addition, even youth workers who favor keeping competition out of youth meetings admit that it can be a powerful motivator. "If you want something done in the short term, competition is the way to go," says one youth minister. "Wave a free pizza in front of my group, and they'll do almost anything."

"Competition is a great incentive," adds Steve Fitzhugh. "I think one of the reasons the Fellowship of Christian Athletes has enjoyed so much success is that much of what we do is built on the platform of competition and games."

Finally, competition is probably the best way to turn a bland game into an exciting and fun group experience. "I think competition is absolutely necessary in making a game fun," explains Wayne Rice. "Competition is what motivates kids to play well, to use all their energy, and to creatively accomplish a goal. You want games that demand maximum energy and deliver maximum fun. The only way to get that is with competition."

So what's the problem with competitive games?

Well, competition is a double-edged sword that often cuts both ways. Although it makes games fun for winners, it can be miserable for losers. Thom Schultz observes: "Some games have a competitive element, and that's fine. Everyone leaves the experience with his or her self-esteem intact. Kids enjoy the experience, and there are no hard feelings. If that's the outcome, competition is OK. But if it produces hard feelings, someone takes it too seriously, or the desire to win overshadows the desire to just have fun—then competition begins to produce results that aren't all positive."

In short, competition does have its place in youth ministry, but only when it's used carefully, like the "fire" that it is. But competition isn't the only game in town. You can balance competitive games with cooperative games.

Cooperative Games

Cooperative games are group-centered. They're games in which everyone participates and no one wins unless *everyone* wins. There are no losers, because everyone contributes to the group's success. These games stress things such as interdependence, relationship building, and communication. The value of the game is primarily in the process of playing, not in the end result.

Cooperative games are harder to design than competitive games, but they're always worth the effort. David Rahn explains: "In youth ministry you're looking for an immediate stimulation element, and competition generally provides it. With cooperation you have to work harder to make the experience attractive. But it's so exciting to see kids of different skill- and ability-levels cheering each other on. That enables you to make applications such as being the body of Christ or loving one another."

Controlling the Fire

It's your decision whether to use competitive games, cooperative games, or some of each. But if you use competition, keep in mind the following guidelines. They'll help you make sure that your kids have healthy fun and don't end up with negative memories of your group— or of you.

1. Stay out of the game.

Darrell Pearson suggests that adults are the most frequent cause of competition getting out of hand. "I don't let them play," he states flatly. Adult volunteers can umpire, lead cheers, or do the wave, but keeping them out of the fray tends to keep competition manageable. Remember that the games are primarily for the kids, not for you.

2. Monitor kids' feelings.

Walt Mueller recommends that competitive players monitor their feelings as they participate by asking questions such as "How do I feel about my opponent?" "How do I feel about myself?" or "Am I treating people with love and respect?" If competitive urges start to overshadow Christlike love, you might want to stop and take an attitude check.

3. Keep competition in check.

"Any game that has ceased to be fun for even one person in your group," observes Walt Mueller, "has crossed the line." Perhaps the score has become so lopsided that one team has no hope of winning. Spontaneously award them a zillion points. Or change the rules. It's up to you how to do it, but do something. Don't leave any victims on the playing field. It's better to stop the game early than to let kids walk away thinking, "I'm no good."

4. Keep the stakes low.

At times competition becomes unhealthy because kids care more about winning than about playing the game. So make the prize for winning something small. "It's vital to make the game itself more important than who wins," says Wayne Rice. "So it's not a good idea to promise the winners free camp registration and make everyone else pay. But if you win the egg and armpit relay, so what? Are you going to go around *bragging* about it? Who cares if you got 10,000 points? What are you going to do with them? The object is to have fun. You want to make winning almost anticlimatic."

5. Enjoy the game.

Your attitude toward the game is vital, for kids will pick up on and follow your lead. "Entering into the experience with a spirit of fun and adventure takes the edge off a competitive game," observes Rich Mullins. "The pressure isn't just to win. Rather, you're invited to participate and to enjoy. Consequently, success and failure don't have any meaning."

6. Make sure competition fits your objectives.

"Before I use competition," explains David Rahn, "I want to know that the learning outcome lends itself naturally to competition. For example, competition around Scripture scares me." If a competitive game doesn't fit your lesson, create a cooperative game to help kids learn what they need to know. Likewise, David Rahn reminds us that "if your goal for the game is mixing, mingling, and having fun, the type of game you play—and the spirit in which you play it—will be different from when you gather kids to play basketball against another youth group."

7. Remember *why* you're playing.

"Games in the church aren't about winning," says Jim Burns. "You want to give kids a positive experience that relates to their faith. I like games because they give kids a memorable, positive impression of the church, that Christians can have fun." Games should also help kids develop character. Walt Mueller observes: "You can win and be a loser. You can lose and be a winner. It's all about character."

So which is better: cooperative games or competitive games? It depends. It depends on the game, on your kids, on how well you keep perspective when competitive juices run high, and on what you want to accomplish with a game.

Whichever style of game you favor for your next meeting, we've got you covered. The rest of the chapter alternates cooperative and competitive games (a concrete reminder to balance cooperation and competition) and then tops it all off with a game that can go either way. Use the games that follow to help your kids have fun and learn crucial lessons about doing one's best and working for the common good.

Amoeba Crawl cooperative game
Jim Burns

Game Summary: Kids will complete an obstacle course while tied together.
Game Supplies: You'll need long pieces of rope (or twine) and an obstacle course.

The Game:

Before kids arrive, set up an obstacle course. The obstacles can be as simple as chairs to weave around and doorways to go through or as complex as pews to go over and under, a stepladder to crawl under, and a set of stairs to navigate. Other obstacles might include a table to go over and under, a flagpole to go around, or a closet to go into and out of.

When kids arrive, have them form teams of five to ten. Have members of each team huddle together and lift their arms above their heads. Then tie a rope around the waists of the members of each team, making sure not to tie it so tightly as to hurt anyone.

Explain that the challenge of Amoeba Crawl is for team members to travel around the obstacle course while tied together. Team members can't untie themselves or endanger any member of the team. And everyone on a team must navigate the course and cross the finish line for the team to finish the course. Walk through the obstacle course so kids know exactly where they're supposed to go. Then tell kids to decide as a team who will lead, who will be in back, and how the team will proceed.

Have teams complete the course one at a time. Encourage teams to cheer and encourage each other as they complete the course. When every team has finished, ask the entire group the following questions:

★ **What did you enjoy most about this game? enjoy least?**

★ **What strategies helped your team complete the course?**

★ **What things worked against your completing the course?**

★ **What are real-life situations that demand cooperation?**

Variation idea

To add an element of competition, time teams as they go through the obstacle course. Then have kids discuss how they need to cooperate with others when they compete in real life. Ask kids to describe times they need to balance cooperation and competition. To close, have kids brainstorm ideas for balancing the two in real-life situations.

★ *Broom Hockey* competitive game
Dave Stone

Game Summary: Kids will use brooms and a chalkboard eraser to play an indoor game of hockey.

Game Supplies: You'll need two brooms, one chalkboard eraser, and twenty-two chairs.

The Game:

Form two rows of ten chairs each. Make sure the chairs face each other and the rows are four feet apart. Set one chair at each end of the rows. (See diagram.)

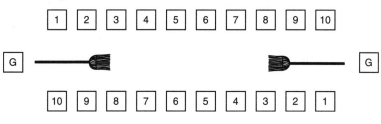

Form two teams of ten or fewer. If there are an uneven number of kids in the group, ask for a volunteer to act as referee or to play on two teams. If there are more than twenty kids, form multiple teams of five to ten and have teams take turns playing each other. Ensure that everyone gets an equal chance to play by having each team play every other team.

Have members of each team sit in one row of chairs. If you have fewer than ten on a team, either leave several chairs empty or remove the empty chairs from the row. Then number players as indicated in the diagram, making sure that kids remember their numbers and that you have two players for each number. Finally, place a broom at each end of the rows and a chalkboard eraser in the center of the rows.

Explain that Broom Hockey is played much like regular ice hockey except that Broom Hockey has these special rules:

All-Star advice

The easiest way to make sure everyone is on a winning team is to rearrange teams periodically—even during the middle of the game. Switching teams around takes the sting out of losing since at one time or another everyone is on the winning team.

★ Each team's home goal is the chair between the rows on that team's right.

★ Goals are scored by sweeping the eraser through the front legs of the opposing team's goal (chair).

★ When you call out a number, kids with that number are to grab the brooms by their goals and attempt to sweep the eraser through the opposing team's goal.

★ Players may not lift their brooms off the floor—no slap shots or high sticking!—or body check their opponents.

★ If anyone breaks the previous rules, the opposing player gets an uncontested shot from center ice (halfway down the row).

★ Seated players are to turn their feet sideways, heel to heel, to keep the eraser in play, but they cannot block the goal.

★ If the eraser goes out of the playing area, you'll drop it between the players for a face-off at the spot it escaped.

★ After each round, the brooms and the eraser will be returned to their original positions.

Answer any questions and repeat the rules as needed and then begin the game by calling out a number between one and ten. Keep calling out different numbers until everyone has played at least one round.

Hippity-Hop cooperative game
Jill DeCesare

All-Star advice

Whether you're using a cooperative or a competitive game, rig teams to get the results you want. Walt Mueller, for example, recommends deliberately pairing up kids who aren't getting along to force some relational dynamics. "If two kids aren't getting along," he suggests, "put them on the same team so they have to work together." Rigging teams can also coax "fringe" kids into the thick of an activity where they can get to know kids who are more likely to reach out. Finally, if someone invites a friend to a meeting or a retreat, make sure that the youth group member and his or her friend aren't separated too early.

Game Summary: Kids will cooperate with each other as they compete in an expanding "three-legged race."

Game Supplies: You'll need eighteen-inch lengths of twine (or string), scissors, and masking tape.

The Game:

Have kids form teams of four to six. As much as possible, be sure teams have equal numbers of members. Use masking tape to create two lines on opposite sides of the room, at least five feet from the walls. Ask team members to line up single file behind one line, with at least five feet between teams.

Have the first two members of each team stand side by side and then tie their inside ankles together with a piece of twine. Tell kids that Hippity-Hop is a cooperative race in which team members must race to the other line and back. However, every time members of a team return to the starting line, they must tie on another team member and race down and back again. Teams will continue until each team has completed the course with all of its members tied together.

Ask if there are any questions and then begin the race. When everyone is finished, distribute scissors so team members can cut themselves free. Then have the entire group discuss the following questions:

★ **Why did teams seem to slow down toward the end of the race?**

★ **How is this like what happens in real life? How is it different?**

★ **What enabled your team to successfully complete the course?**

★ **What can this teach us about working effectively with others?**

Hot Shots competitive game
Andy Hansen

Game Summary: Kids will attempt to shoot Finger Blasters through toilet seats.

Game Supplies: You'll need two toilet seats (or Hula Hoops), twenty Finger Blasters (ten of each color), and masking tape.

The Game:

Use the masking tape to create two lines: one down the center of the room and one at a right angle to the center line and fifteen feet from the wall. (See diagram.)

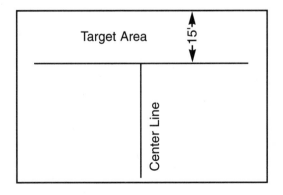

Target Area

15'

Center Line

All-Star advice

Finger Blasters are eight-inch rubber band-propelled foam missiles. They're available from RecSource—(503) 254-3030. Ask them to send their free Finger Blaster Flight Instructions sheet that contains more than a dozen games using Finger Blasters.

All-Star anecdote

Andy remarks, "If someone is a really bad shot and a Finger Blaster goes into the other team's territory, it's awfully hard to convince those people not to bite, step on, and pretty much destroy it before they pass it back." You may want to encourage teams to trade stray Finger Blasters back and forth.

Have kids form two teams. If you have an uneven number of kids, ask someone to act as scorekeeper. Assign teams to opposite sides of the center line, and give each team ten Finger Blasters. Ask each team for two volunteers to stand in the Target Area in front of their teams. Give one volunteer from each team a toilet seat, and instruct him or her to stand no more than three feet from the wall. Tell the two other volunteers that they are to retrieve and shoot back their teams' Finger Blasters so they can be fired again.

Explain that the goal of Hot Shots is for team members to shoot their Finger Blasters through their toilet seats and hit the wall in front of their Target Area. Kids holding the toilet seats can move as needed to guide Finger Blasters through, but they must not move more than three feet away from the wall. A team earns ten points for every successful shot. Shots that miss the toilet seat or go through the toilet seat without hitting the wall do not count. Team members cannot leave their playing area to retrieve stray Finger Blasters, but the two "retrievers" may go anywhere in the Target Area to recover the team's Finger Blasters. Of course, retrievers can touch and return only their team's Finger Blasters.

Assign one youth or adult volunteer to keep track of each team's score. Play for a predetermined length of time or until one team has scored one hundred points. If you decide to play again, ask teams for new volunteers to work in the Target Area.

Variation idea

Hot Shots also works well with foam footballs. You can even adapt it for use with a large group seated in an auditorium or worship area. Hang toilet seats across the stage. Form teams by "drawing" an imaginary line down the center of the audience. Tell kids that they must remain seated and that shots count no matter which toilet seat a football goes through. Finally, have each team's onstage volunteer retrieve and throw back his or her team's football.

Kings of the Mountain cooperative game
Les Christie

Game Summary: Kids will work together to see how many of them can fit onto or into a specific space.

Game Supplies: No supplies are required.

The Game:

Ask kids how many of them have played King of the Mountain. The idea of that game is to see who can claim the top of a pile and then kick and throw off any challengers. Explain this is a cooperative version of King of the Mountain. Instead of seeing how many people one person can toss off, the goal is to see how many kids can simultaneously stay on top of or in a certain space.

If there's snow outside, have kids create a huge snow-pile and try to get everyone in the group on top. No snow? No problem. Select one or more of these warm-weather variations and proceed!

★ Sofas can hold far more people than you might expect. The usual safety concerns about keeping the sofa firmly planted on the ground apply—but any sofa that's made it into a youth room has pretty much sagged to capacity already.

★ How many kids can fit into a phone booth? Note: Do not close the door! For an even greater challenge, use a cellular phone to call the booth after your kids have packed themselves in! (You got the number first, didn't you?)

★ How many kids can get at least part of their bodies into a Hula Hoop? Count fingers, toes, ears—whatever. Better yet, how many kids can fit inside a Hula Hoop so that their bodies don't touch the ground outside? Encourage kids to link arms to hold each other in the Hula Hoop.

★ If you're really adventurous, take your group on a hike or climb that will require kids to help each other make it to the top.

☆ All-Star advice ☆

Kings of the Mountain is a great example of how a slight change in rules can turn a competitive game into a cooperative one. Use your imagination to transform other competitive games your kids enjoy into cooperative and fun learning experiences.

☆ All-Star anecdote ☆

David Rahn and a group of high school football players stood at the base of a mountain in the Grand Tetons. Their goal—make it all the way to the top.

They hiked up to a base camp, and the night before their ascent they decided that either all of them would make it to the top or that none of them would. The next morning they packed their gear and headed up the trail, but it quickly became clear who was aerobically fit and who wasn't.

Rahn explains: "The defensive backs didn't have any trouble with the altitude, but the linemen were huffing and puffing. Finally, about a hundred feet from the top, one of the big linemen sat down and said: 'That's it. I can't go any further.' Immediately, the defensive backs sat down and said, 'We're not going either.'

"That big lineman wanted to wring their necks, but he couldn't catch them. He told them they could pick him up on the way back, that it didn't matter…but the other guys were insistent: It was either *all* of them or *none* of them.

"After a few minutes, he silently got up and bitterly began trudging up the hill. He was angry. But when the team finally made it to the top, nobody celebrated like the kid who had sat down. It was a great team effort."

Marauder competitive game
Bart Campolo

Game Summary: Kids will work together to form letters, numbers, shapes, and symbols.

Game Supplies: You'll need a tall platform or stepladder to stand on. (You can even stand on the church van or bus.)

The Game:

Have kids form teams of six or more. Explain that you will call out a letter of the alphabet, a number, a shape, or a symbol and that team members are to line up in that shape as quickly as possible. For example, if you call out "A," team members should line up to create the two long lines and one short line of an A. If you call out "7," kids should line up to form the one long line and one short line of a 7. Teams must form letters, numbers, and symbols so the "bottom of the page" is closest to you, but they can form shapes however they want.

Tell kids that you'll view their efforts from your lofty perch and award various points for speed, accuracy, and general style. Answer any questions kids have and then climb to your "viewing stand." Call out a letter of the alphabet and see which team forms it first. Keep kids on their toes by alternating between letters, numbers, shapes, and symbols. Keep the game competitive by awarding points generously to teams that are lagging behind. If your

All-Star advice

Bart Campolo maintains that just about any game can be made more attractive by giving it a cool name. For instance, few teenagers will want to play Simon Says, but they're intrigued by Sinister Hypnosis. It's basically the same game, but it has a drastically increased "cool factor." So give your games a boost by slightly altering the rules and giving them new and cool names.

kids become really good at this game, consider adding more complex shapes and symbols.

People Pyramid cooperative game
Thom Schultz

Game Summary: Kids will learn and practice cooperation as they construct human pyramids.

Game Supplies: You'll need a camera to take instant photos.

The Game:

Have kids form groups of ten. Tell groups their goal is to create human pyramids. Ask for three volunteers to help demonstrate how this can be done. Have two of the volunteers get down on hands and knees next to each other and then have the third volunteer get on hands and knees on top of and straddling the other two volunteers.

Thank the volunteers for their help and then tell kids that no more than four group members can touch the ground after a pyramid has been formed and that each pyramid must stay standing for at least fifteen seconds. Capture the moment for posterity by taking instant photos of each pyramid.

For an extra challenge, ask kids to complete various tasks while they're still in their pyramids. For example, have the person on the left end of the bottom row take off his or her shoes, the person in the middle of the second row feed bananas to the kids below, both members of the third row turn completely around, or the person on top try to throw a foam ball into a wastebasket.

☆ All-Star ☆ advice

Give teenagers a chance to opt out of this activity because of either health concerns or inappropriate dress. Also, choose a soft place to do this activity—either on a grassy lawn or on mats.

Variation idea

If your group is not large enough to form two groups of ten, have groups of five form pyramids. Tell kids that only three group members may be touching the ground after a pyramid has been formed.

Quarterdeck Quickstep competitive game
Rick Bundschuh

Game Summary: Kids will attempt to "stay on board" in this fun version of Simon Says.

Game Supplies: You'll need only a large open space in which to play.

The Game:

Divide your playing area into three sections. If you're outside, use jump-ropes or pieces of string to create the lines. Make the sections like those in the diagram, placing them about fifteen feet apart.

★ All-Star advice ★

According to Rick: "This game has all the best elements of any game I've ever played. It's active, guys and girls are on equal footing, and you don't have to be all that fast—you just have to pay attention. And the same person seldom wins twice."

Tell kids that the three sections are actually three "decks" of a ship. The section on the left is the poop deck, the center section is the main deck, and the section on the right is the quarterdeck. When you call out the name of a deck, kids are to get into that section as quickly as they can, because the last person into a called deck is out of the game. In addition, if you call out the name of a deck kids are in and they step out, they're out of the game.

Have everyone start on the main deck—the center section. Then call out decks until only one person is left in the game. (If you have a large number of kids playing, you'll want a spotter to help determine who's the last person onto a deck.) To make the game more difficult, keep kids guessing by pointing to the quarterdeck as you call out the poop deck!

Sardines cooperative game
Rick Houston

Game Summary: Kids will play a cooperative variation of Hide and Seek—and get really well-acquainted in the process!
Game Supplies: No supplies are required.

The Game:

Gather your group in a central area, and ask for two volunteers to go hide together. Explain that everyone else is a Seeker. Seekers are to stay where they are for three minutes and then set out to find the hiding pair.

Here's the catch. When someone finds the kids who are hiding, he or she must join them in the hiding place. This will continue until everyone is crammed or "sardined" into one spot. So encourage the kids hiding to select a small, cramped space such as a closet or the area beneath a stairway.

You can send out Seekers individually or in pairs. Pairs are safer if you have security concerns, but beware of sending out mixed-gender pairs. If you send out a dating couple, they might not be located for hours!

If the church board catches you using this game, suggest that it's a practical way to get your kids acquainted with the entire facility!

Save the Sailor competitive game
Michael D. Warden

Game Summary: Team members will toss "lifesavers" over the heads of "drowning sailors."
Game Supplies: You'll need bicycle inner tubes (or Hula Hoops), fifteen-foot lengths of light rope, and masking tape.

The Game:

Before the meeting, inflate the inner tubes. Then tie one piece of rope to each inner tube. Use masking tape to create a long line down the center of the room.

Form equal-sized teams of four or more. Instruct teams to line up behind the masking tape line. Then have each team select a Sailor

all-star games from all-star youth leaders

⭐ All-Star advice ⭐

Choose teams at random, recommends David Stone. "Don't have kids count off by twos because they'll automatically start moving around to get in the right positions." Instead, have kids draw team colors or team numbers out of a hat. The goal is to form teams without having anyone chosen last or feeling he or she is second best. "Walk in and start moving kids around," suggests Dave. "Rearrange them as a group, but don't call on them individually."

```
    X        X        X        X

  ↕ 10'
  ─────────────────────────────────
    •        •        •        •
    •        •        •        •
    •        •        •        •
    •        •        •        •
    •        •        •        •
```

other team members will try to rescue. (It's best if Sailors don't wear glasses or contacts.) While kids are deciding, use the masking tape to make Xs ten feet from the line and opposite the teams. (See diagram.)

Instruct Sailors to stand on the Xs opposite their teams. Explain that other team members will take turns attempting to throw their lifesavers (inner tubes) over the heads of their Sailors. Teams will earn one hundred points for every "save." After each toss, the next team member in line is to reel in the lifesaver and make his or her attempt. Stepping over the line cancels out a toss. Tell Sailors that they must keep their arms at their sides and at least one foot on the masking tape X at all times.

If kids understand the rules, begin the game. Continue play until everyone has had three or more tries. (If you notice that kids aren't doing very well at saving Sailors, move the Xs closer to the line.) Reward the winning team by allowing them to choose the next game.

extension idea

Draw out the meaning of this game by asking kids to answer these questions:
★ How did you feel when you successfully saved your Sailor? when you missed?
★ How is this game like trying to tell people about Jesus? How is it different?
★ What should we do to reach others for Jesus as effectively as we can?

Trust Walk cooperative game
Walt Mueller

Game Summary: Kids will lead each other through an obstacle course to experience what it's like to be responsible for someone else—and to depend on someone else.

Game Supplies: You'll need one blindfold for every two teenagers and an obstacle course.

The Game:

Before the meeting, plan out or prepare an obstacle course. Use chairs, tables, wastebaskets, halls, stairways, or the pews in your worship area to create a course that winds throughout the building. Or plan out an outside course that leads kids around your building or to a specified location.

Have kids form pairs and then give each pair a blindfold. Ask pairs to decide who will be the Leader and who be the Follower. Explain that partners will take turns leading each other blindfolded through the obstacle course. Followers may not peek to see where they are going, and Leaders must do all that they can to guide their Followers through the course without incident or injury. Leaders should warn their Followers of approaching steps, low doorways, chairs, or any other hazards. They should also physically guide their Followers as necessary. Stress the Leaders' responsibility to make sure that their Followers arrive at the goal safely.

Instruct Leaders to blindfold their Followers and to direct them safely through the course. When the Followers complete the course, have partners exchange roles. Allow these new Leaders to follow a different course back to the starting area.

For an extra challenge, have pairs complete specific tasks. For example, you might ask one pair to walk to a nearby convenience store to

☆ *All-Star* ☆ advice

Safety should always be a consideration, but it's especially crucial for this game. Make sure the blindfolds are clean and do not contain residue from cleaning solution. Also, avoid taking kids up or down sharp-turning stairways without handrails or leading kids too close to traffic.

Variation idea

You can modify the Trust Walk in various ways. For example, tell Leaders not to speak but to lead only by hand. Or add "distractors" who will attempt to confuse Followers with incorrect instructions and warnings. You might conduct your trust walk in a wooded area where kids will need to be guided over fallen trees and along winding paths.

buy a can of cat food and another pair to retrieve the third hymnal from the fourth pew from the front of the worship area.

After both partners in each pair have been Followers, ask the entire group the following questions:

★ **What were you thinking while you were being led? leading?**
★ **What did you find difficult about being led? about leading?**
★ **What makes it hard for you to trust? What makes it easier?**
★ **Who do you trust to lead you? Why do you trust this person?**
★ **Why do you think we can trust God's leading in our lives?**

Ultimate Relay competitive game
Susie Shellenberger

Game Summary: Kids will race to see who can complete an obstacle course fastest.

Game Supplies: You'll need a stopwatch, high-energy music to play during the relay, and an obstacle course.

The Game:

Before the meeting, create an obstacle course in a gym or a large outdoor area. What you include in the obstacle course is limited only by your imagination, but you might want to start with the following ideas:

★ Furniture gauntlet: Set up two parallel rows of chairs in an "S" formation. Instruct kids to run between the rows without touching the chairs. Whoever touches a chair must return to the beginning and try again.

★ Jump-rope jig: Tell kids they must each jump-rope ten times. Jumps can be cumulative—they do not have to occur all in a row.

★ Basketball shoot: Challenge kids to shoot a basketball (or a foam ball) through a basketball hoop. (You can also use a wastebasket if you don't have access to a basketball hoop.)

★ Crazy crawl: Instruct kids to crawl under boards lying across two rows of chair seats.

★ Vertical tunnel: Have kids place a Hula Hoop over their heads and twirl it down to the floor.

★ Tire tracks: Set two rows of five tires each next to each other. Make sure the tires in each row are one foot apart. Tell kids they must step inside each tire as they run through the course.

★ Bat heads: Use masking tape to create an X on the floor. Place a baseball next to the X. Explain that kids are to place the large end of the bat on the X, put their foreheads on the small end, and run around the bat once without letting it fall or touching it with their hands.

Have kids form teams of eight or fewer. Explain that teams will race against the clock (and each other) to see who can complete the obstacle course fastest. Teams will go through the course one at a time, and the team with the fastest time wins. The only other rules are that kids must complete a station before advancing to the next one and that racers can't advance until the team member ahead has completed his or her station.

If everyone understands the course and the rules, start the music and the game. Encourage kids to cheer for everyone, not just members of their own teams. Be sure to time teams to find out which one truly is fastest.

All-Star advice

Warn kids ahead of time to dress appropriately for this event. Ask everyone to wear gym shoes and jeans. In addition, no matter how tempting it may be, do not succumb to requests for shopping-cart relays and the like. It takes only one skin-scraping, bone-breaking accident to turn your game time into a disaster.

Unbeatable Frisbee Golf competitive and cooperative game
Tiger McLuen

Game Summary: Kids will toss Frisbees in a game of golf that can be either cooperative or competitive.

Game Supplies: You'll need one Frisbee for every three kids, masking tape, markers, and an outside area in which to create a course.

The Game:

Before the meeting, create a "golf course" by selecting various targets in your playing area that kids can toss Frisbees at. Keep in mind that Frisbees can break glass but bounce harmlessly off street signs, trees, dumpsters, and the like.

Plan each golf hole by selecting a starting point (such as the second step in front of the building) and determining a target (such as the open garbage can behind the bush on the Third Street side of the building). Assign a par score for each "hole"—a challenging but reasonable number of throws that it takes to get a Frisbee from the

All-Star advice

"I think the idea of games as cooperative is wonderful, but for us to pretend that competition doesn't exist or to think that any and all competition is the enemy is unrealistic. Dealing with competition is a skill that every kid has to learn. If we don't allow kids to interact with that skill *within* the Christian context and *with* adult Christian modeling, we're assuming they'll know how to handle competition out in the world. That just doesn't work."—
Tiger McLuen

starting point to the target.

You might even plan "water traps" into the course by turning on sprinklers where Frisbees are likely to land. Kids will have to go into the spray to retrieve and throw their Frisbees. Make the game more challenging by using metal wastebaskets as targets for some holes and requiring kids to get the Frisbees *inside* the wastebaskets. Tape or nail tin pie-pans to trees for some targets or place a Hula Hoop on the ground and require kids to get the Frisbee completely within the hoop. A section of flagpole marked with masking tape or ribbon makes a challenging target, too!

Place a seven-inch piece of masking tape on the bottom of each Frisbee. Finally, decide whether this game will be cooperative or competitive—it can go both ways!

Ask kids to form teams of three. Give each team a Frisbee and a marker. Then explain the rules of the game. The basic rules for the cooperative and competitive versions of Unbeatable Frisbee Golf are the same:

★ Team members must take turns tossing their team's Frisbee at each hole.

★ Frisbees must be played where they land unless this involves danger—for example, going into the street or onto the roof.

★ If a Frisbee can't be played where it lands, you will assess a one-stroke penalty and the Frisbee must be played from the closest safe location.

★ After playing a hole, each team must mark on the masking tape on the bottom of its Frisbee how many tosses it took to complete the hole.

If you're going to play the cooperative version of this game, tell teams that they must rotate or switch Frisbees with another team after each hole. After the last hole, teams will total the number of tosses recorded on the bottoms of the Frisbees. Declare the Frisbee with the fewest tosses the winner of the game.

If you decide to play the competitive version, simply have teams keep their Frisbees throughout the game. The team with the fewest number of tosses wins.

Games That Make a Point

*I*f life were perfect, you'd always be able to find the ideal game to complement any lesson—a game that took no preparation, required no supplies, and ended with your kids stampeding out the door to put great spiritual truths into practice.

But life isn't perfect. Sometimes you'll need to adapt ready-made games so they fit your specific group. Now and then you'll even need to create your *own* games.

Don't panic! Creating games that make profound spiritual points isn't as hard as it first appears...*if* you follow the simple four-step process described here. Let me show you how to do it.

1. Start with a specific learning goal in mind.

In one sentence, what is it you want your kids to discover during this lesson? If you can't state the main idea or point of the lesson in one sentence, chances are your kids won't be able to either.

Sometimes you'll want to design a clever, fun game that your kids will love—and there's nothing wrong with that. But how much better it would be to design a game that makes a specific, lesson-related point! Remember, you want your kids *learning*, not just entertained.

So write your lesson idea or point on an index card and keep it in view as you create your game. Try to narrow your focus to a single, specific idea—otherwise, you're likely to miss it.

2. Decide what emotional response you want from your kids.

Kids participate more enthusiastically and learn more effectively when their emotions are engaged. So make sure your game elicits an appropriate emotional response.

For example, you might want kids to end the game feeling curious, challenged, frustrated, confused, thoughtful, anxious, hopeful, smug, joyful, appreciative, cautious, awe-struck, or some other appropriate emotion.

Select the emotion that's appropriate for setting up a discussion of your lesson idea. If you'll be talking about Jesus' forgiveness, set up a game that helps kids experience compassion. Considering how to share the Christian faith? Find a way to make your kids feel a little uncom-fortable.

Once you've decided on an emotion, add it to your index card.

3. Design an experience that evokes this emotional response.

The easiest way to "create" a game is to adopt one that already exists. For example, use a game such as In or Out (p. 61) when you want to teach a lesson on cliques or a game such as Lap Sit for a meeting on trust (or the lack thereof).

If you prefer, you may want to adapt or modify an existing game so it creates the desired response. For example, if you wanted kids to learn compassion for the sight-impaired, you could alter Tower of No Babbling (p. 68) so that blindfolded teams could talk as they built their towers.

Whether you adopt, adapt, or create your own game, make sure you get everyone involved in a emotion-evoking experience that will lead kids to discover for themselves the point of the lesson.

4. Write questions to help kids clarify what they've learned.

This step will help you ensure that kids have thought about what they experienced. Asking kids to discuss what happened, how they felt about it, and how the experience illustrates or reinforces your learning point will cement the point into kids' minds and hearts.

In most cases, kids will discuss their opinions and feelings more freely in small groups. Then you can simply ask volunteers to report their groups' responses. Moreover, open-ended questions (those that can't be answered with a simple "yes" or "no") will challenge kids to really think about their answers.

If your group is not used to talking about what they think, expect to spend some time helping them learn this skill. You might want to get kids started by always selecting a person in each small group to begin sharing. For example, ask the person closest to you or the person wearing the most green to start. Finally, make sure you always ask groups to report their insights to the rest of the group. This will give kids another chance to feel heard and allow you to monitor what meaning your kids have taken out of the experience.

Creating games that make a point takes time, but it's worth the effort it takes. It enables you to incorporate game time into the overall learning experience. So give it a try—by trying out some of the following games!

ALL-STAR GAMES FROM ALL-STAR YOUTH LEADERS

Bigger and Better games that make a point
Jim Burns

Game Summary: Kids will trade eggs for bigger and better items to learn about what matters and why.

Game Supplies: You'll need one egg for every four kids.

The Game:

Before the meeting, recruit one adult volunteer for each team of four kids.

Have kids form teams of four. Give each team an egg. Make sure that each team has a watch and then synchronize the watches. Explain that each team is to trade its egg for something bigger and better and then trade the bigger and better item for something even bigger and better.

Teams will have thirty minutes to make as many trades as they can, each time for something bigger and better. Teams may go from house to house, stop people on the street, or do anything that's safe and reasonable to make their trades. Teams will be accompanied by adult leaders who will make sure their trades are legitimate.

Before teams leave, explain that they must be back within thirty minutes. Any team returning after the thirty-minute deadline will be disqualified, so teams need to pace themselves. The adult going with each team will neither speak on behalf of the team nor make sure team members return in time.

Send teams out to "wheel and deal" for thirty minutes. When teams return, ask them to present their biggest and best items. Encourage teams to describe how they traded up for their final items. Then ask the adult leaders to decide which object is, in fact, biggest and best. The judges' decision is final.

> ### ☆ All-Star ☆ anecdote
>
> Game contributor Jim Burns reports: "We played this game at my daughter's birthday party. The boy's team came back with an old sofa, a toilet, and an umbrella. The girls had a skateboard ramp—which sat in front of my house for a week."

> ### ☆ All-Star ☆ advice
>
> One way to spice up a game is to turn it into a bit of a challenge or a contest. Wayne Rice explains: "You can motivate kids with the idea of trying to succeed at something—to come out with the most, best, longest, fastest, or whatever." Add reasonable competition to make the game interesting and challenging.

After congratulating all the teams for their efforts, have team members discuss the following questions. After each question, ask for volunteers to report their teams' answers. Ask:

★ Which object did you hate trading away? Why did you trade it away?

★ What did someone trade that surprised you? Why do you think this person traded it?

★ How is this game like trading our old life for new life in Jesus? How is it different?

Character Scavenger Hunt games that make a point
David Bryant

Game Summary: Kids will hunt for disguised characters in a public place and then discuss disguises they use in real life.

Game Supplies: You'll need copies of the "Character Descriptions" handout (pp. 72-73), photographs of your characters without disguises, tickets, disguises for your characters, prizes, and refreshments.

The Game:

Thorough planning is required for this game. The actual game is quite simple, however. You place disguised characters in some public place and challenge kids to find them.

Several weeks before the game, recruit five or more adults to be your characters. Take a photograph of each actor, and give him or her a character description. You can use the character descriptions on pages 72-73 or use your own. Explain that actors are to dress their parts and do nothing to draw attention to themselves. An actor can stand at a pay phone, eat in a restaurant, or shop in a store. But each actor must be in an approachable place where kids can easily see and ask him or her if he or she is one of the actors. Whenever an actor is discovered, he or she will give the discovering team a ticket. Instruct your actors to meet you at your meeting place exactly five minutes after teams are to return. Finally, you'll also need to recruit one adult volunteer to accompany each team.

> ### ★ All-Star ★ advice
>
> If you use actors your kids know, be creative. For example, put a tall man in a wheelchair so his height doesn't give him away. Use wigs, glasses, and costumes to make discovery a challenge.

Once you have characters assigned, choose a public place where kids can search for them. You might consider an amusement park, a crowded mall, or an airport. (Given the increased security in most airports, you might want to choose another location.) Whatever the case, try not to attract the attention of security people or you may be calling parents to arrange bail money.

To begin the game, instruct kids to form small teams of three to five. A large group of marauding teenagers may frighten people who aren't a part of the game, but there's safety in numbers. Explain that the goal of the game is for teams to identify as many characters as they can in the specified time. (An hour works well for a large mall.) Teams will collect one ticket from each character they locate, and the team with the most tickets at the end of the game wins.

Make sure that kids also understand the following rules:

★ Team members must stay together and be accompanied by an adult monitor at all times.

★ Each team will elect an official timekeeper, who is responsible for getting the team back to the meeting place by the specified time. You will subtract one ticket for every minute a team is late.

★ Kids may not run or be rude. Adult monitors may penalize teams one or more tickets for infractions.

★ When a team approaches a possible actor, one team member must say, "Hi. Are you (name of character)?" (Have kids practice asking the question.) If they've guessed correctly, the team will receive a ticket. A team may get only one ticket from each actor.

Before kids leave, synchronize teams' watches and remind kids of the time limit.

When everyone has returned, total each team's tickets and declare a winner. Award fun prizes such as sets of Groucho Marx-style costume glasses to members of the winning team. Applaud the characters for their performances. Then invite kids to relax, swap stories, and enjoy refreshments together. At some point during the discussion, ask the entire group the following questions:

★ **What was the funniest moment of the scavenger hunt for you?**

★ **What was the most embarrassing moment of the hunt for you?**

★ **What made it easy to spot the characters? What made it hard?**

★ **What "disguises" do we wear in real life? Why do we use them?**

★ **What are the dangers and benefits of using "disguises" in life?**

★Clay Creations games that make a point
Walt Mueller

Game Summary: Kids will create miniature sculptures to represent their relationships with God.

Game Supplies: You'll need molding clay or Play-Doh.

The Game:

Ask kids to form groups of three. Give each group one ball of clay or a half-can of Play-Doh. Instruct kids to take turns in their groups creating sculptures that portray their relationship with God and then showing those sculptures to each other.

Tell kids they will each have sixty seconds to create a sculpture. Then the other two group members will have sixty seconds to guess what the sculpture represents. If no one guesses correctly in sixty seconds, the sculptor should tell or reveal what it is.

After each sculpture has been identified, encourage the sculptor to answer the following questions:

★ **In what ways does your sculpture represent your relationship with God?**

★ **If you could change any part of your relationship with God, what would it be?**

After trio members finish explaining their sculptures, ask them to roll the clay into a ball so the next person can have a fresh start to make his or her sculpture.

When everyone has finished explaining his or her sculpture, have trios discuss the following questions. Ask:

★ **What was the hardest part about doing this exercise? the easiest part?**

★ **In what ways were your sculptures similar? How were they different?**

★ **What did this exercise teach you about someone in your group? about yourself?**

★ **How is showing and then destroying our sculptures like how we share deep feelings?**

Variation idea

This game is easily adapted to fit almost any topic! Consider asking kids to mold sculptures representing how they feel about themselves, their families, their parents, school, church, or the youth group. If you're really brave, ask kids to mold sculptures portraying how they feel about you!

Clear the Electric Fence games that make a point

David Rahn

Game Summary: Kids will learn to cooperate with each other as they work together to clear a hurdle.

Game Supplies: You'll need enough string to stretch tightly between two trees or across a doorway.

The Game:

Relax…it's an imaginary electric fence! The goal of this game is for teams of teenagers to get up and over a string. For the team to win, everyone on the team must clear the string.

Establish an imaginary "electric fence" by stretching a length of string or twine between two stationary objects. Place the fence four and one-half feet above the ground and then have kids form teams of four people each. (If you can arrange to play this game outside over soft earth, that would be best.)

Explain that team members must figure out how to get everyone on the team up and over the "fence" without touching it—lest they be electrocuted! Teams can use whatever they can find to help as long as it's safe, but they may not launch anyone over the fence!

If everyone understands the rules, challenge teams to clear the fence as quickly and safely as possible. When everyone has cleared the fence, ask the entire group these questions about the issues of cooperation and interdependence. Ask:

★ **How did working with a team make clearing the fence easier? How did it make it harder?**

★ **What did you like about having to depend on others to clear the fence? What**

All-Star anecdote

David Rahn hadn't been a youth worker long when he tried this game during an overnight hike with his group. "I'd seen the game once and thought I could do it on the spur of the moment," he explains. "So I tied a little rope between two trees, but I hadn't paid close enough attention to how *high* you ought to tie the rope. I was acting as wise, crafty teachers do and not giving the kids help. Whenever they asked a question, I'd challenge them to figure it out for themselves. Then, before I knew what was happening, they picked up the smallest guy there and threw him like a javelin over the rope. He landed wrong—and broke his arm. I think the moral of this story is not to play any game without thorough and proper planning."

Variation idea

To increase the challenge of this game, assign team members different restrictions such as "You have a broken leg" or "You're unconscious."

didn't you like?

★ **How is this game similar to being a member of this group? How is it different?**

★ **In what ways do you depend on others to help you succeed? In what ways do others rely on you?**

Copycat games that make a point
Walt Mueller

Game Summary: Kids will be challenged to observe carefully, listen well, and explain themselves clearly as they try to copy a geometric design.

Game Supplies: You'll need poster board, a marker, paper, pencils or pens, and writing surfaces.

The Game:

Before kids arrive, draw a simple geometric design of overlapping circles, squares, and triangles on poster board. Place it face down in the center of the room so no one in the group sees it before the game begins.

Form equal-sized teams of three or four. Set up chairs, one row for each team, as illustrated in the margin. Turn the chairs closest to the poster board so kids seated in them can see it. Turn the other chairs facing away from the poster board.

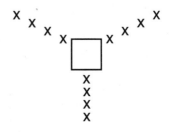

Instruct each team to sit in one of the rows. Give the person on the end of each row (farthest from the poster board) a sheet of paper, a hard writing surface, and a pencil. Explain that each team is to create an accurate copy of the diagram at the center of the circle. The catch is that only the team member at the center of the circle will see the diagram. That team member must whisper instructions for drawing the diagram to the second person in line, who will whisper them to the next person, and so on until the person at the end of the line receives them. Then that person is to draw on the paper whatever he or she has been told to draw.

Allow three-member teams ten minutes to draw. Allow more time if you're using a complex diagram or if teams have four members. The task is nearly impossible if there are five kids on each team.

When time is up, compare each team's finished diagram with the original. Then ask the entire group the following questions:

★ **How accurately did your team reproduce the original geometric diagram?**

★ **Why didn't you create an exact copy? How did you get as close as you did?**

★ **What communication skills did you need to use to succeed at this task?**

★ **What can this game teach us about how we should communicate with others?**

Variation idea

Create a sculpture out of toothpicks and gumdrops and then cover it with a towel. Give the kids at the ends of the lines toothpicks and gumdrops. Then challenge teams to create exact replicas of your sculpture.

In or Out games that make a point
John Sanny

Game Summary: Kids will experience what it's like to be excluded as they scramble to form different-sized groups.

Game Supplies: No supplies are required.

The Game:

Explain that kids are to mingle around talking with each other while they wait for you to call out a number. Then, when you call out a number, kids are to form a group that has that number of people in it and hold hands with their group members.

Everyone who doesn't land in a group of the right size is out of the game and must stand at the edge of the room with his or her back to the group. Call out numbers between three and five until you have only three players remaining. Then call out "two" to bring the game to an end.

To help kids learn from their experience, challenge them to form pairs and trios as quickly as possible—but without excluding anyone. Then have partners and trio members discuss the following questions. Ask:

★ **How did it feel to be excluded? to exclude others from your group?**

★ **How is this game like what happens to you in your day-to-day life?**

★ **How is this game like what happens in our group? How is it different?**

★ **What can we do to make sure we always include everyone in our group?**

extension idea

For extra fun, gather twenty- to twenty-five shoe boxes or other small boxes before class. Then have group members write the barriers to inclusion on the boxes. Stack the boxes to give a powerful visual of just how high the walls within the group might be. Then read Ephesians 2:13-14 and knock down the wall so kids can see exactly what Jesus Christ has done.

Family Night

Instant Family games that make a point
G. Keith Olson*

Game Summary: Kids will practice healthy communication skills as they resolve conflict between "family members."

Game Supplies: You'll need paper, pencils, and photocopies of the "Instant Family" handout (p. 74).

The Game:

This game works with groups of five or five hundred—whatever size crowd you can reasonably control. It's also a great game to use when kids and parents meet together. Adults will experience how it feels to be a teenager, perhaps not getting a voice in decision making. Teenagers playing adult roles will discover what it's like to take adult considerations into account.

Arrange players into groups of four and five. Be sure participants aren't with members of their own family. Ask groups to form circles facing inward. Announce that for the next thirty minutes each group will become a family.

Then assign family roles. (Because roles are assigned without regard for age or gender, an adult may play a teenager or a teenager may play an adult.) In groups of five, the person whose birthday is closest to Christmas will be the father. The person whose birthday is next closest will be the mother. The person with the next-closest birthday will be a

*Adapted from a communication game designed by Keith Olson.

thirteen-year-old daughter, the person with the next-closest birthday will be a seventeen-year-old son, and the remaining group member will be a fifteen-year-old daughter. In groups of four, omit the role of the father and assign the other roles as previously described.

Encourage participants to have fun with the game and their roles but to be realistic. A thirteen-year-old daughter has very real concerns in any family meeting, so participants playing that part should attempt to represent those concerns. A parent has concerns, too, and participants playing parents should keep those concerns in mind.

Explain that families will work together to solve a problem or to make a decision. In the process, participants will practice problem solving and communication skills, experience what it's like to be in different roles within the family, and gain insight into the pressures other family members may feel. Tell families that they have twenty minutes to resolve their issues, after which they'll all discuss their experiences.

Give each family a sheet of paper and a pencil. Then present each family with one of the situations on page 74 (or other situations you have created).

Remind families that they have twenty minutes to resolve their issues. Then give five-, three-, and one-minute warnings so groups can wrap up their discussions.

When time is up, ask families to report their conclusions to the rest of the group. Then ask group members to discuss the following questions. After each question, ask for volunteers to report their groups' answers. Ask:

★ **What skills or approaches helped you resolve your problem?**
★ **What tended to block your family from resolving your issue?**
★ **What did this game teach you about family communication?**
★ **What did you learn about other family roles from this game?**

Lap Sit games that make a point
Michael D. Warden

Game Summary: Kids will experience what it's like to be supported by others—and to support others.

Game Supplies: No supplies are required.

The Game:

You'll need at least eight participants for this game. Ask kids to form a large standing circle with their right shoulders facing the center of the circle. Have kids inch closer to the center of the circle, which will cause them to squeeze together. Keep moving them closer together until everyone's toes are touching the heels of the person in front of him or her. It's very important that everyone be close together!

All-Star advice

You might want to consider breaking girls and guys into two groups for this game. At the very least, be sensitive to how your kids are dressed.

Explain that, when you give the signal, everyone is to sit back on the lap of the person behind him or her. This should form a circle of kids sitting comfortably on each other's laps.

Make sure everyone understands and then give the signal. If it doesn't work the first time, try again. In most cases, kids weren't standing close enough together. If everyone sits down together, kids should be able to maintain this position for some time. You may even want to challenge kids to "walk" forward or backward while they're in the sitting position.

While kids are still sitting, ask them the following questions:

★ **What's it like to have someone support you? to support someone else?**

★ **What do you think would happen if one person decided to walk away?**

★ **How is this circle like how we support each other? How is it different?**

★ **How do others support you in daily life? How do you support others?**

★ **What's one practical thing you can do to support someone else today?**

Mall Mayhem games that make a point
Les Parrott III

Game Summary: Kids will observe how others react to "abnormal" behavior at the mall.

Game Supplies: You'll need pencils and index cards.

The Game:

Take your group to a crowded mall during a busy shopping season, such as prior to Christmas or before kids go back to school. (You may want to alert the mall of your plans beforehand. Some malls restrict this type of activity.) Gather kids outside the mall, and have them form trios.

Give each trio a pencil and several index cards. Be sure that each trio has a watch and that watches are synchronized so everyone can return to the central meeting place at the same time. Then send the trios into the mall on a mission: to see how people respond to them when they act abnormally.

Explain that one trio member is to act abnormally while the other trio members observe from a distance how people respond. Direct the watching members to record their observations on index cards. Encourage each trio member to take a turn at acting abnormally.

Emphasize that kids can do anything abnormal as long as it's not illegal, harmful to others or themselves, or dangerous. If kids have difficulty thinking up ideas, suggest the following possibilities:

★ Sit down next to—not on—a bench in a public area.

★ Stand on one foot for an extended period of time.

★ Pretend to read a book while holding it upside down.

★ Carry on a conversation with a piece of merchandise.

Remind kids of when they need to be back and then send them out on their missions of mall mayhem.

When kids are back together, ask them to

⭐ All-Star ⭐ anecdote

Dr. Parrott reports: "A girl in one of my classes did this at school. She went into another class on campus and simply sat next to her chair instead of in it. It drove people nuts. We learned that just the tiniest difference is seen as abnormal."

Variation idea

Consider linking the behaviors to a specific holiday or to the time of season you play the game. For example, if you lead the game at Easter, require behaviors to relate to the Easter Bunny. Require Santa or reindeer themes around Christmas or kindergarten costumes at back-to-school time.

65

describe what they did and how people responded to them. After everyone has shared, have kids vote with their applause for the most outrageous behavior, the most subtle behavior, the most creative behavior, and the funniest response elicited.

Then ask the entire group the following questions:
* ★ **How do people respond to someone who's different?**
* ★ **How did it feel to be viewed as abnormal by others?**
* ★ **How do you tend to treat people who are different?**
* ★ **How can we make everyone feel welcome in this group?**

Miracle at Midnight games that make a point
Steve Fitzhugh

Game Summary: Kids will take a gently discomforting walk in the dark and be surrounded by silence—maybe for the first time in years.
Game Supplies: You'll need flashlights and a sack.

The Game:

This game works best on a reasonably clear night, preferably one with a full moon. Lead kids on a "nighttime nature walk," away from civilization. You'll want to go to a campground, a park, a forest, or another area that's open and away from city lights. (If you use this game on a retreat, list "Miracle at Midnight" on the itinerary, but don't explain what it is.)

Around 11:30 p.m., stop the walk and ask kids to stand in a circle. Pass around the sack to collect all the flashlights and watches. Then lead kids slowly and carefully toward the open area where you'll be stopping at midnight. Since you'll have the only watch, you can stop at approximately midnight—no one will know the difference!

When you get to the open area, tell your group that it's time for a "miracle at midnight." Have kids stand in a circle and then explain that the miracle will be sixty seconds of total silence. Lead the group in a few practice

★ All-Star advice ★

"My personal philosophy is that I want to create a moment," says game contributor Steve Fitzhugh. "Every now and then, someone will look back and say, 'That sermon or song changed my life.' In my life there are different moments that I have been able to grow from, and that's what I want to create for students. I want them to look back and say, 'Wow! That was meaningful.'"

"miracles": a ten-second period and then a thirty-second period. Give kids time to work through their giggles, to get settled, and to brush off any bugs.

Emphasize that you're serious about the silence and that you don't want anyone ruining the experience. You want absolute silence. Then count down from ten to the beginning of your minute.

"What happens then," explains Steve, "is that all of a sudden you can hear the crickets blaring and cows mooing in the distance. And at the end of a minute, I break the silence by saying, 'The miracle at midnight is this: How many of you can see better now than when we first turned off the lights?' Then kids realize that they can see one another even without the flashlights."

Use this game to set up a brief talk about how we can hear God's voice or see God in action when we spend time silently before him. It also works well to introduce discussions of how seldom we truly rest in the Lord or discussions of biblical passages that talk about God being praised in his creation.

Strike It Rich games that make a point
Steve Fitzhugh

Game Summary: Kids will discover what they really value in life by realizing how hard they'll work for a very little bit of money.

Game Supplies: You'll need twenty one-dollar bills and one five-dollar bill.

The Game:

Before your kids arrive, hide the bills in the meeting area. Take extra care to make sure the five-dollar bill is particularly difficult to find.

When kids arrive, ask the entire group to call out things they can buy for one dollar. Then ask them what they could buy for five dollars. Encourage kids to list all the things they would buy if they had that money in hand. Then ask kids what they would be willing to do to get one dollar and to get five dollars.

After several minutes of discussion, ask for everyone's complete attention—you have an important announcement to make. Explain that you have hidden twenty-five dollars in the room—twenty one-dollar bills and one five-dollar bill—and that kids can keep any money they find within the next five minutes.

★ All-Star ★ anecdote

Steve Fitzhugh describes how this game looks in action: "Talk about chaos! Chairs are flying, and kids are all over—searching everywhere they can. They want to get that money!"

After five minutes, instruct kids to stop searching and to return to their seats. If they didn't find all the money, retrieve what's left and put it away. Then have kids form trios, and ask trio members to discuss the following questions.

★ **How do you feel about your effort to discover the money?**

★ **Do you think God would be jealous of the effort you put forth?**

★ **How do you feel about the effort you invest into finding God?**

★ **What could you do to seek God more passionately than you do?**

You can extend the point of the game by following it with a lesson on seeking after God or God's will.

Tower of No Babbling games that make a point
Joani Schultz

Game Summary: Kids will silently work together to build towers in order to learn the importance of communication.

Game Supplies: You'll need gumdrops, plastic bags, toothpicks, and a yardstick.

The Game:

Before the game, make one "construction kit" for every five kids. Put thirty gumdrops and thirty toothpicks in each bag. Make an extra bag with only thirty gumdrops.

Instruct kids to form groups of five. Explain that members of each group will work together to build as tall a tower as possible. Towers must be free-standing—groups may not lean them against walls or support them in any other way. Also, every group member must contribute to the building effort. Kids have ten minutes to complete their towers, after which you'll measure all the towers to determine whose tower is tallest. The only catch is that there must be no verbal or written communication. All work must proceed in complete silence.

Answer any questions and then give the signal for total silence. Give each group a construction kit, which is to remain unopened until you give the signal again. When every group has a kit, give the signal for groups to begin building.

Give five-minute, three-minute, and one-minute warnings. After you signal the end of ten minutes, measure the height of each tower. Then declare a winner, and present the extra bag of gumdrops as the Tallest Tower Trophy. Suggest that groups dismantle and eat their towers as they discuss the following questions:

★ **What did you like about this experience? What didn't you like?**

★ **How did you work together as a group? How could you improve?**

★ **What did this game teach you about yourself? about your group?**

★ **Were you more comfortable being a leader or a follower? Why?**

★ **How was this game like being part of this group? part of a family?**

All-Star advice

Your signal can be a whistle, flashing the lights, or sharply clapping your hands twice—but make sure your signal is clear and distinct. And be sure everyone understands what your signal is before you begin this game.

Wobble Fall games that make a point
Thom Schultz

Game Summary: Kids will take turns being supported by and passed around a standing circle.

Game Supplies: No supplies are required.

The Game:

Explain to your teenagers that this game involves some risk—so if participants don't take it seriously, someone could be hurt.

Ask kids to form groups of six to eight members. It's crucial that each group not be larger than eight. Otherwise, physics and gravity will sabotage your efforts. You'll see why in a moment.

Have groups form standing circles, facing inward. Then ask for a volunteer Wobbler to stand inside each circle. Have everyone else in a circle tighten the circle by standing shoulder-to-shoulder around the Wobbler.

Ask Wobblers to cross their arms over their chests, stand with their

feet together, and lock their knees. Demonstrate the correct posture, as illustrated in the margin. Emphasize that Wobblers must keep their knees locked or else their circles won't be able to support them while they're wobbling. In addition, direct kids in a circle to stand with one foot slightly behind the other and to hold their hands in front of their chests in a "catching" position.

Then carefully explain the following sequence for the Wobble Fall experience:

★ To begin, Wobblers will assume the Wobbler posture, close their eyes, and ask "Ready?"

★ If everyone in the circle is in the catching position, the circle is to respond "Ready!"

★ If everyone in the circle has responded "Ready!" Wobblers are to ask "Fall?"

★ If everyone in the circle is ready for the Wobbler to fall, circle members are to answer "Fall!"

★ The Wobblers are then to fall in any direction—with eyes closed and knees locked. Circles are to slowly roll the Wobblers around, gently and carefully handing the Wobblers from person to person.

Explain that no one is to talk or laugh while the Wobblers are being passed around. Then, after Wobblers have gone around the circles two times, they are to be carefully set back up straight.

To make sure everyone understands, help one circle demonstrate the sequence and process. Then have all the circles go through the sequence and pass their Wobblers around. When circles finish, have them select new Wobblers and repeat the sequence and the process. Continue until everyone has had a chance to be a Wobbler. If someone is hesitant to be a Wobbler, explain that although the game looks threatening, it's worth the risk.

When everyone has had a chance to be a Wobbler, direct groups to break into pairs or trios. Then have small-group members answer the following questions:

★ **How did you feel about having to rely on others for support?**

★ **What was it like to be responsible for**

All-Star advice

Be sure the circles are shoulder-to-shoulder and small. The larger the circle, the farther Wobblers have to fall and the heavier they seem when they fall. Small, tight circles will help equalize size differences between Wobblers and Catchers.

not dropping someone?

★ How is this activity like or unlike being in a group of friends?

★ What's one way you've been supported by someone else lately?

★ What's one way members of this group can support each other?

Character Descriptions handout

Johnny Q. Public

A former spy for a federal agency, John entered the Witness Protection Program several years ago. He used his training in disguise and espionage to disappear into thin air, but he's found one trait hard to break. He frequently jingles the change in his pocket.

Sara Sensational

You may remember Sara from the television commercials she did a few years ago. Sara went to Hollywood convinced she would become a legend, but she never quite rated her own star on the Walk of Fame. In fact, those deodorant commercials are about the only acting she ever did. Now she lives in the past—still convinced she's glamorous.

Harley Harriett

Buying that "road hog" was the best thing Harriett ever did. Sure, it was expensive and everyone thought she would end up as the hood ornament on a Mack truck. But the thrill of the open road, the feel of wind in her hair—it makes life worth living. If only she didn't need to keep her stupid job as a surgeon to support her motorcycle mania.

Dennis the Daredevil

Dennis has climbed Mount Everest, wrestled alligators, and parachuted. He also thinks bull riding is for sissies. His latest adventure was in Japan, where he tried to teach sumo wrestlers a thing or two. His friends think he's the most swaggering, arrogant guy they know...but what can they say? He *can* do anything.

Character Descriptions handout

Evie the Effervescent

When you think expressive, energetic, and engaging, you're thinking of Evie. She moved here from southern Italy a year ago and brought with her a flair for fashion and expression. She's the life of every party she attends because she loves talking with people—anyone, at any time.

Arnie the Accountant

What an organized, orderly guy! He even irons his socks! But Arnie's friends from the Flaxton School of Business Law would be amazed to see him after hours. That's because, although he is a mild-mannered, toe-the-line bean counter by day, he goes a little crazy when the sun goes down—as the master of ceremonies at the local alternative-rock club!

Instant Family handout

★ Discuss and decide on a family policy regarding curfews. Who, if anyone, should have one? When should curfews be? What happens if someone misses his or her curfew? Are there any exceptions? If so, what are they? What is the purpose of curfews?

★ Discuss and decide on a family policy regarding dating. What are your family's standards governing dating? Do the daughters have the same rules as the son? At what age may dating begin? What sort of dating is permissible? What role does a parent have in monitoring dating?

★ Discuss college and come to a family understanding about each child's participation. Will the kids go to college? Why or why not? If so, which college will each person attend? Who will pay for college? How will it be paid for? Will students live in a dorm, at home, or in an apartment? What role does a parent have in monitoring grades and attendance? What if someone wants to drops out?

★ Decide where you'll go on a family vacation. The vacation will take you away from home for three weeks. Where will you go? How will the vacation affect your schedules? How much money will you spend? How will you travel?

Off-the-Wall Games

You've planned a life-changing lesson. You found exactly the right music to drive home the point of the lesson. You even have a pretty good idea what you'll say during closing prayer. So why add a game to the mix?

"Games break down the walls so kids don't have their defenses up," observes Bob Stromberg. "After a game, kids are ready to do something else—to sing, to participate, to share in a small group. The walls have been broken down during game time."

Will you have visitors at your meeting? kids who aren't frequent attenders? If so, you'll want to get them connected with the group—and games, especially off-the-wall games, can help!

These games don't require loads of verbal interaction; they don't require kids to divulge information about themselves. They're a low-risk, high-fun way to bring new kids on board—and to get everyone's attention. In addition, if you plan to lead a hard-hitting Bible study, an off-the-wall game will lighten up the meeting. At the very least, an off-the-wall game will help kids relax and enjoy each other. So use these and other off-the-wall games, but keep the following tips in mind as you do so.

1. Make sure kids know it's OK to have fun.

If your group isn't used to playing games, especially in church, an off-the-wall game may feel sinful. ("Laugh? In *church?* What if God sees us?") If this is true of your group, bring your kids along slowly, saving the outrageously fun games for later. You may even want to go outside to play off-the-wall games. Kids may feel that God doesn't care as much if they get rowdy outside.

2. Use games to burn off adolescent energy.

The impact of hormones and adrenalin on adolescent behavior is well-documented, so use these games to burn off kids' surplus energy *before* you start Bible study. Spending ten minutes of your meeting time playing is a good investment if it helps your kids listen better during the rest of the meeting.

3. Love your church janitor in word *and* action.

Off-the-wall games can be messy, so always plan ahead to ensure easy cleanup! In fact, consider turning postgame cleanup into a bit of a competition. That way you can serve your janitor *and* teach your kids a fun way to be responsible at the same time.

4. Keep surplus grungy clothes on hand.

If you're going to do something that involves water balloons, mud pies, or some other dry cleaner-friendly substance, make sure there are extra clothes around. Oversized shirts and extra gym shoes are a good start. You might also ask a few regular attenders to bring extra sets of clothes to loan to kids not dressed for game time.

5. Make off-the-wall games an occasional treat.

A steady diet of anything gets tiresome. Off-the-wall games are no exception. Use them sparingly, and they'll have maximum impact. To get you started, try the following time-tested, way-fun, off-the-wall games!

Blackout Musical Chairs off-the-wall games
Miranda Farrell-Myers

Game Summary: Kids will play a fun game of Musical Chairs…in the dark!

Game Supplies: You'll need chairs and music.

The Game:

Play this game in a completely dark room. If you can't darken your meeting area, have kids play blindfolded.

Set up a circle of chairs, all facing out. Place one less chair in the circle than you have kids in the game. Tell kids that they'll be playing Musical Chairs…with a twist. Unlike regular Musical Chairs, this version is played in the dark.

Ask kids to form a circle around the circle of chairs and to stand with their arms folded across their chests. When the music starts, kids are to march slowly around the circle in a clockwise direction while maintaining the crossed-arm position. When the music stops, kids will have five seconds to find a chair. Anyone still standing or sitting on someone else when the lights come on after five seconds will be eliminated from the game.

If everyone understands the rules, turn out

Variation idea

Place kids inside a circle of chairs that are facing in. Use one less chair than you have kids. Have one person stand in the center of the other kids. The goal is for the person in the middle to get into an empty chair when the music stops. Because everyone is moving when you turn off the music, the empty chair appears for a fraction of a second—and then shifts again.

the lights and start the music. After each round, have each eliminated player take one chair from the circle, place it away from the circle, and sit in it—neither speaking nor participating. Tighten the circle of chairs and play another round. Be sure to vary the length of time you play the music from round to round. Play until only two people remain.

To help kids learn from their experience, have them form small groups and discuss the following questions:

★ **What about this game did you enjoy most? What did you enjoy least?**

★ **How did it feel to be excluded when you were eliminated from play?**

★ **How is this like an experience you have had at school or with friends?**

Controlled-Insanity Inside Baseball off-the-wall games
Peter Knudsen

Game Summary: Kids will enjoy a great game of baseball—and you don't even need to find a grassy field!

Game Supplies: You'll need four paper plates, masking tape, and a large foam ball and bat.

The Game:

It's a favorite national pastime, but sometimes it's hard to come up with nine players on a side. Relax. Now you can play with as few as four or as many as twenty players on a side. And you won't even need a baseball!

☆ All-Star ☆ advice

One word of advice from our game contributor: "Don't play this game around a fish tank." He declined to offer any further explanation.

Clear a room. Use the paper plates to mark four bases, with about thirty feet from home plate to second base. Then tape the plates to the floor.

Have kids form two teams, with equal numbers of guys and girls on each team. Explain that Controlled-Insanity Inside Baseball is played like normal baseball, with the following exceptions:

★ There are no home runs, because balls are played off the walls.

★ There is no sliding into bases, wearing of spikes, or spitting.

If everyone understands the rules, have teams stand on opposite sides of the room. Spin the bat on the floor between the two teams—the team that the head of the bat is closest to when it stops gets to bat first.

Play as many innings as time allows. If one team starts winning by a large margin, declare the game over and choose new teams.

Corner Shuffle off-the-wall games
Michael D. Warden

Game Summary: Kids will hustle from corner to corner to tell you what they really think.

Game Supplies: You'll need four Hula Hoops, a portable stereo, and tapes or CDs with four styles of music (see p. 79).

The Game:

Gather kids in the middle of the room. Explain that kids will be making choices about what they prefer and that they will be voting for their choices with their feet. When you ask a question, kids will have five seconds to hustle to the corner that best represents their answer to that question.

☆ All-Star ☆ advice

This game forces participants to make choices. Consider adapting it for use with lessons on ethical choices. Present an issue and several possible solutions and then ask kids to choose and defend one. You might require kids to stay in their original corners and then eliminate the corner with the fewest kids after the five-second period. This will help kids experience the tension between doing what they believe is right and following the crowd.

As you read the choices, kids may shift from corner to corner—but they will have just five seconds to make their final selections after you read the fourth option. Anyone not in a corner five seconds after the fourth choice has been read is out of the game. Your decision is final regarding who will be eliminated from the game.

At the end of each round, give every corner a chance to defend the superiority of its position. Place a Hula Hoop on the floor near each corner and designate it the Speakers Circle. Anyone in a corner who wants to persuade kids in other corners to switch can hop into the circle to state his or her case. Quickly rotate through the corners, giving each corner one minute or less to make its pitch. After each corner has presented its case, allow kids five seconds to shift to another corner if they want to. Then eliminate the corner with the fewest kids in it.

Ask the following questions, directing kids to move to different corners depending on what they decide. You'll need to be very clear, pointing out which corner represents each choice.

Round One: Which leisure-time activity do you enjoy most?
1. Hanging out with friends
2. Watching television
3. Talking on the phone
4. Listening to music

Round Two: Which style of music is your favorite? (Play a brief selection from each of the following styles.)
1. '60s rock
2. Classical
3. Gospel
4. Country

Round Three: Given a choice, which food would you prefer to eat all the time?
1. Pizza
2. Hamburgers
3. Tossed salad
4. Frozen yogurt

Round Four: When you first awake in the morning, which animal do you most resemble?
1. A grizzly awakening from hibernation
2. A busy beaver
3. A cheerful songbird
4. A slow-moving sloth

Round Five: What was your last trip as a youth group (to camp, a retreat, a concert, etc.) like?
1. A thrilling roller coaster ride
2. A grueling trek through a swamp
3. A mysterious trip full of surprises
4. The vacation of a lifetime

Round Six: If you could pick any spot to enjoy a week's vacation, where would you spend it?
1. Your own house
2. A sunny beach
3. The mountains
4. A chocolate factory

Variation idea

Turn this into an icebreaker by having kids introduce themselves and explain their answers to kids standing in different corners after each round.

Fire Brigade off-the-wall games
Thom Schultz

Game Summary: Teams will use squirt bottles to try to extinguish their candles.

Game Supplies: You'll need masking tape, candles in holders, aluminum foil, squirt bottles full of water, matches, and a whistle.

The Game:

Form teams of three to five. Count out as many candles as there are teams. Set the candles in a line, putting each candle on a large piece of aluminum foil and making sure candles are at least two feet apart. Use the masking tape to make a line parallel to and fifteen feet away from the line of candles.

Ask teams to line up behind the masking tape line opposite their candles. Give the first person in each line a squirt bottle. Tell kids they will use their squirt bottles to extinguish their candles. Kids are not permitted to squirt at each other, and they must hand the squirt bottle to the next person in line whenever you blow the whistle. Then the person who was squirting will go to the end of his or her team's line.

If everyone understands the rules, light the candles and start the game. Blow the whistle often so there's plenty of frantic action. The winner is the team that extinguishes its candle first. Play a second round in which teams try to extinguish other teams' candles.

Variation idea

Inflate balloons and put a glob of shaving cream on each balloon. Then position one team member holding a balloon in the place of each candle and ask teams to squirt the shaving cream off the balloons being held by their teammates.

Heads-Up Basketball off-the-wall games
Rick Houston

Game Summary: Kids will play a mean game of basketball—without baskets!

Game Supplies: You'll need a foam ball, masking tape, and a watch.

The Game:

Clear a large room of furniture. Form two teams of six to sixteen kids. Have each team choose one person to be a Basket. Position the Baskets where the baskets would normally be on a basketball court. Use masking tape to create a line on the floor that gives at least six feet of clearance around each Basket.

Explain that the goal of this game is to score points by hitting the opposite team's Basket. Teams score two points every time they hit the opposing Basket *below the shoulders*. Baskets can duck or raise one leg to avoid shots, but they can't move from their spots or raise their hands above shoulder height.

Tell kids that they must remain stationary when they have the ball. They can move the ball only by passing it. In addition, if someone "fouls" an opposing team member, you'll deduct two points from the team of the person who committed the foul. Finally, if someone enters either of the six-foot safety zones around the Baskets, his or her team will lose four points.

All-Star advice

A word from our game contributor: "Even better than foam balls are Koosh Balls that have air bladders in them. They're worth a thousand times what they cost because you can throw them at full force from five feet away and they don't hurt the person being hit."

Decide how much time you have to play the game and then divide the game into two halves. You may want to have teams choose different Baskets for each half. If everyone understands the rules, enjoy the game. It works well either inside or outside!

Mall Hide-and-Seek off-the-wall games
Joani Schultz

Game Summary: Kids will try to avoid being tagged while they cruise the mall.

Game Supplies: No supplies are required.

The Game:

Take your kids to a local mall. Before you turn them loose, explain that this game is played like regular Hide-and-Seek except that kids don't really hide. They are to walk (not run!) around the mall and try to avoid getting tagged. (You may want to alert mall authorities of your plans.)

You'll be It to begin the game, but anyone you tag also becomes It and can tag others to make them It. After a while, kids won't know who's It so everyone will have to watch out for everyone else.

Explain that kids cannot leave the mall or run in the mall—anyone breaking either rule is automatically It. Kids can "hide" in any public place—behind a fountain, in a telephone booth, behind a rack of clothes, in a corner booth at the food court—but every five minutes they must find a new location. Encourage kids to remain calm at all times and to be courteous both to shoppers and to mall personnel.

Take kids to the center of the mall. Challenge them to try to avoid being tagged for one hour, after which time they are to return to the center of the mall. If everyone understands the rules, send kids out, giving them a three-minute head start before you start searching for them.

At the end of the game, lead the entire group to the food court for an impromptu "party." Invite kids to swap stories about the best and worst places they hid.

Variation idea

To make hiding more difficult, require kids to hide in pairs. This offers the added benefit of keeping kids together for the sake of safety.

Night Crawlers off-the-wall games
Jill DeCesare

Game Summary: Kids will try to elude youth leaders in the darkness of the night.

Variation idea

Increase the game's difficulty by challenging kids to capture a flag, to move a log from one end of the playing area to the other, or to complete some other task without being caught. You can also play the game in the church or some other large building.

Game Supplies: You'll need flashlights, dark clothing, camouflage face-paints, and whistles.

The Game:

Decide on and mark boundaries for a playing area during daylight hours. A park or a wooded area works particularly well. If you spot fences, dangerous marshes, poison ivy, or other hazards, do not play this game there! Finally, designate a central location to be the "holding pen."

Recruit several adult volunteers to be Taggers. Instruct them to come dressed in dark

82

clothing. Before the game, ask Taggers to apply camouflage makeup. Give each Tagger a whistle and a flashlight. (Do check the batteries first!)

Introduce the Taggers to the group. Explain that Taggers will have twenty minutes (allow longer for groups larger than twenty) to tag all the kids in the group by shining a flashlight beam on them. When kids are tagged with a flashlight beam, they are out of the game and must return to the holding pen.

Kids may hide anywhere they want, but they cannot climb trees or buildings, get into water, touch other players, attempt to knock the flashlight from a Tagger's hand, or otherwise endanger anyone in the game.

You will use quick whistle-blasts to signal the beginning and end of the game. Kids must return to the holding pen as soon as the game ends. Otherwise it will be assumed that they're lost or lying injured in the woods. One long whistle-blast means that someone is hurt and everyone is to come out of hiding. Taggers will respond to the site of the whistle. If someone sprains an ankle or is otherwise hurt, he or she should say so loudly and repeatedly. The closest Tagger will then sound a one-blast alarm and find the injured party. Anyone who yells out a false injury-report is out of the game.

All-Star advice

Think safety—but don't be terrified to try things. Learn to think like a lawyer. Once you've planned a game, ask yourself: Is there anything dangerous about it? Could someone conceivably get hurt? Is there an element of the unknown in the game? Ideally, you can answer yes to all three questions. If you can't, you've designed a terminally boring game.

On the other hand, don't take unnecessary risks. Some games are just too dangerous to play. (Shopping-cart relays come to mind.) And you need to minimize the risk of injury by making sure playing surfaces are appropriate and safety gear is worn when necessary. Don't do anything stupid. Ask yourself: Would I play this game if the pastor and all the parents were watching? If you can answer yes to that, you're probably safe. *Probably.*

Warn kids that Taggers won't shine their flashlights all the time, so they should expect to be surprised. If everyone understands the rules, give kids a five-minute head start to go hide. Then blow two quick blasts to start the game and send out the Taggers.

Pile-Up off-the-wall games
Joanne Knittle

Game Summary: Kids will pile up on each other's laps—for a reason!
Game Supplies: You'll need sturdy chairs.

The Game:

Place chairs in a circle, one chair for each member of your group. Instruct kids each to sit in a chair. Explain that you will read a list of instructions that kids are to follow if they fit into the category described. For example, if you say, "Shift two seats to the right if you were born in Cedar Rapids, Iowa," everyone who was born there would move two chairs to the right, while everyone else would stay put. This will create "piles" of kids in some chairs and leave other chairs empty.

Try to alternate between instructions that apply to everyone and those that apply to only some kids. Think up your own categories to personalize the game for your group or use the following ideas to get you started:

★ **Move two chairs to the left if you are wearing blue.**
★ **Move one chair to the right if you have ever visited Alaska.**
★ **Move five chairs to the left if you've studied a foreign language.**
★ **Move three chairs to the right if you know all the verses of "The Star-Spangled Banner."**
★ **Move one chair to the left if you have ever played a game of chess.**
★ **Move two chairs to the right if you know when my birthday is.**
★ **Move two chairs to the right if you gave me a birthday present.**
★ **Move three chairs to the left if you've ever been told to clean your room.**
★ **Move one chair to the left if your room is a mess right now.**
★ **Move five chairs to the right if you would rather have a salad for lunch than tacos.**
★ **Move one chair to the left if you have passed a lifesaving course.**

Variation idea

Instead of arranging chairs in a circle, place them in rows, with equal numbers of chairs in a row as there are rows. Then have kids move forward, backward, left, right, or some combination of forward-left or backward-right. If someone is in the front row, he or she would go to the back of the row to move "forward," while kids on the sides would start at the other side if they couldn't move as instructed.

★ **Move ten chairs to the right if you enjoy bowling.**
★ **Move ten chairs to the right if you have ever owned a pet.**
★ **Move one chair to the left if you've ever been in a foreign country.**

End the game by having kids take turns answering the following question:

★ **What's one set of instructions that would have let you move but not anyone else?**

Pop Goes the Santa off-the-wall games
Rick Bundschuh

Game Summary: Kids will race to blow up balloons and stuff them in Santa Claus suits and then count the balloons as they pop them.

Game Supplies: You'll need Santa Claus suits (red long underwear worn backward with the flaps in front work well), 150 small balloons, and a hatpin.

The Game:

Have kids form two teams. Instruct each team to sit together on the floor, and toss each team approximately seventy-five uninflated balloons. Challenge kids to see which team can inflate its balloons (any size they want) and tie them off fastest.

Ask for volunteers from each team. Select three volunteers from each team—*and make sure you have a rather small male from each team in your volunteer pool.* (More about why later.) Designate the small male on each team "Santa," but make the choice appear random so there's no stigma attached to being small.

> ★ **All-Star** ★
> **advice**
>
> When it's time to pop the balloons, you'll be glad you selected small *males* to be the Santas. Still, be *very* careful as you pop the balloons.

When all the balloons are inflated, ask each Santa to get into his costume and face his team. Ask the other volunteers to stand beside their Santa. Then explain that the other two volunteers are Elf Tailors. Their job is to get Santa up to size by stuffing as many balloons as possible into his suit in sixty seconds.

When you give the signal, team members are to toss balloons to the Elf Tailors, who will insert them into Santa's suit. Only the Elf Tailors can stuff the balloons, and team members *must* stay seated while they're tossing balloons toward the Elf Tailors. Finally, all Santa stuffing must stop when you give the signal that time is up.

Play the game, giving thirty-second and fifteen-second warnings and a 5-4-3-2-1 countdown. Then withdraw the hatpin from your lapel (or some other hidden place) and announce that the official balloon counting will begin. Carefully pop each balloon stuffed into each Santa's suit, encouraging teams to count balloons as they pop.

Declare the team that stuffed the most balloons the winner!

Pumpkin Olympics off-the-wall games
Les Christie

Game Summary: Kids will celebrate fall (and cheap pumpkins) with a messy, hose-'em-off Olympic-style competition.

Game Supplies: You'll need pumpkins, shovels, a wheelbarrow, and a dumpster or mulch pile. You'll also need other supplies, depending on the games you choose from below.

The Game:

Timing and planning are critical for this event. Stop by pumpkin patches and grocery stores that sell pumpkins a few weeks before Halloween. Ask the managers if they would like to donate (or sell very reasonably) any pumpkins they haven't sold by Halloween night. Remind them that they'll probably have to pay to have them hauled away and explain why you want the pumpkins. You're almost sure to find all the pumpkins you want for next to nothing. One final word: Don't become enamored with big pumpkins. Small or medium-sized pumpkins are of maximal game-playing value.

The week before your meeting, announce that you're going to hold an Olympic-style competition. However, since every event involves pumpkins in some way, kids should dress in clothes they don't mind getting messy.

All-Star anecdote

Game contributor Les Christie notes that he hasn't added volleyball to the list of games yet, but that doesn't mean you can't.

To begin the competition, form teams of three or four. Challenge teams to think up creative pumpkin-related names for their teams. Then have teams take turns competing in the following events or in other Pumpkin Olympic events that you think up:

Shot Put

Here's the place to use some of the softer pumpkins. Don't worry about marking where the pumpkins land—soft pumpkins have a way of letting you know where they hit.

High Jump

Stack pumpkins as though you're building a brick wall. Challenge kids to jump over the stack without knocking any pumpkins off. Keep raising the stack until you've identified the champion high-pumpkin-jumper in your group.

Relay Race

Have teams compete in a relay race, using pumpkins as batons. To make the relay more difficult, challenge teams to carry two or three pumpkins at a time. You can even combine the relay with an obstacle course and challenge kids to weave in and out of lines of pumpkins or jump over low walls of pumpkins.

Bowling

Use two-liter bottles to create several bowling lanes, ten bottles per lane. Add several inches of water to each bottle to make it more stable. You'll want to forego drilling holes in the pumpkin "balls."

Golf

This is actually croquet, but golf sounds better. Use hockey sticks or croquet mallets as clubs, and create golf "holes" (or hoops) out of untwisted wire hangers.

Juggling

See who can juggle the most pumpkins at once or who can juggle three pumpkins longest. Use small pumpkins only, of course.

☆ All-Star ☆ advice

One way to control competition is to accelerate the scoring. Tiger McLuen states: "I've always believed that, if you're going to play a competitive game, why have someone win five to two when you can have them win five thousand to two thousand? Instead of awarding one point, award five thousand. It communicates that this isn't in-your-face, Super Bowl competition. Properly managed, competition can be lighthearted, and light competition is healthy."

Award points to every team after each event, not simply the winning team or the team finishing second. In addition, vary the points you award to keep competition close throughout. When you've finished every event, challenge teams to clean up the pumpkins as quickly and thoroughly as they can. Award additional points for cleanup efforts. Then total each team's points, and declare a winner.

Sanctuary Foosball  off-the-wall games
Rick Houston

Game Summary: Kids will play a gigantic game of Foosball—within the comfort of the sanctuary!

Game Supplies: You'll need a foam ball or an underinflated beach ball and goals made of large cardboard boxes or PVC pipe.

The Game:

You'll need to play this game in a sanctuary with immovable pews.

With a few simple supplies, you can transform those pews you have always wanted to move into the perfect Foosball table.

Before the game, create goals either by placing large boxes on chairs or by building permanent goals out of PVC pipe. Goals should rise several feet above the pews and be approximately three feet in width.

Have kids form two teams. Then, keeping an empty pew between each row, arrange kids like players on a Foosball table, alternating teams from row to row. If you want to keep the playing area small, place two team members in each row. To create a large area, place one person in each row. Set one goal at each end of the playing area, making sure there is an empty pew between the last row of players and the goal. (See diagram.)

Using a foam ball or an underinflated beach ball, play the game by typical Foosball rules—awarding one point each time a ball goes into or through a goal. Explain that kids can move back and forth along the pews but that they can't jump or leave their pews. If a ball goes

---

All-Star advice

Keep an eye out for useful material (such as PVC pipe) that's being thrown away. One Midwestern youth worker explains: "I know of a local manufacturer that sends sheets of plastic to the landfill all the time. I got some twenty-foot lengths of plastic, turned water hoses on them, and created a water slide. It was great fun." What could you do with cardboard carpet rolls? leaves? car tires? old sofa cushions? The point is: If you find a free supply of cool stuff, look for a way to create a game.

out of bounds, you'll retrieve it and put it back in play where it went out of bounds. Kids can bat or toss the ball, but overhand throws will be penalized one point.

Play a game either to ten points or for ten minutes and then shuffle the teams and play again. Once your kids try this game, they'll love it—so create "permanent" goals out of PVC pipe.

	Goal	
X		X
O		O
X		X
O		O
X		X
O		O
	Goal	

⭐ *Switch Sides* off-the-wall games
Rich Mullins

Game Summary: Kids will play a non-competitive game of dodge ball—sort of.

Game Supplies: You'll need soft rubber balls and a whistle.

The Game:

You'll play this game much as you would regular dodge ball, with a few important changes. To begin, select one person to be the Red Team. Everyone else is the Blue Team. Give all the balls to the Red Team. Explain that when someone gets hit, he or she is not out of the game. Rather, the hit person joins the other team.

Be sure to decide and demonstrate what constitutes a "hit." Is it a hit if the ball is caught on the fly? if it touches the floor first? if it bounces off a wall? if it bounces off another player? Opinions are divided, and "official" rules vary from playground to playground. Try to avoid conflicts by clearly demonstrating the house rules on these issues.

Begin and end play with a whistle blast. (Actually, you could live without the whistle and just flash the lights or clap your hands—but it's great feeling like a big-league coach.) Play until everyone is on one side of the center-court line (which is pretty much impossible) or for five minutes. Play as many rounds as you wish.

Variation idea

Make the game more interesting by tossing in other objects to throw during the game—water balloons, beach balls, or wet sponges.

The Table Game off-the-wall games
Darrell Pearson

Game Summary: Kids will try to defy gravity by crawling around a table-top without touching the floor.

Game Supplies: You'll need a sturdy (check it, please) six- or eight-foot table and a supply of one-dollar bills.

The Game:

Place the table in front of your kids. (It *is* sturdy, isn't it?) Offer one dollar to anyone who can sit on top of the table and then crawl over the edge, under the table, and back up the other side—without touching either the floor or the table legs.

★ All-Star ★
anecdote

Darrell swears there's no ancient Tibetan secret associated with this feat—he's seen it done many ways by many people. He adds, "It takes awhile, and it's usually accomplished first by a female gymnast."

Explain that it's easy to get on the bottom, hanging...but tougher to get back up the other side. Success is often a result of being able to get an arm or leg all the way across the table-top and then pulling oneself around to the top. Remind kids that they can't touch the floor or table legs and that falling is a bad idea.

Position yourself and another volunteer to steady the table. Then challenge kids to give it a try. Give everyone who succeeds one dollar.

Games for Special Days and Events

Sometimes the usual games just won't be right for the situation at hand. Maybe your regular meeting is scheduled around a holiday or some other special time of the year, and you want to play games that relate to that holiday. Or perhaps you've planned a special event, and you're confronted with the challenge (and terror) of leading a crowd of three hundred (or three thousand) kids in a game. What do you do?

Simple. You select or develop games to match your specific needs and situation. For example, if you want to bring out the real meaning of Mother's Day or Father's Day, invite your teenagers' parents to the meeting for "Team Time" (p. 94). Or if your group of several hundred has a little too much energy, lead them in a few rounds of "Wedding Fire Drill" (p. 106).

Whatever you do, keep the following considerations in mind as you select or create a game for your event or holiday. If you do, you're on your way to a sure-fire success.

1. Decide what you want to accomplish with the game.

Is this a just-for-fun game? a game to get kids talking with each other? a game to explore a holiday theme? Think through what you want to do so you can select an appropriate game and place it in the best place in your program.

2. Know your environment—both physically and emotionally.

Physical environment is especially important for special-events games. Where will you play this game? Will kids be moving around? Will the aisles be clear? Will anyone be on stage as you play? What could possibly go wrong with a crowd this large playing the game?

Emotional environment is probably more crucial for special-days games. So be aware of and sensitive to the emotional struggles that many kids face during various holiday seasons and then match the game to your kids' emotional climate. For example, a wild and crazy game is far more appropriate for Groundhog Day than for Mother's Day or Father's Day.

**★ All-Star ★
anecdote**

A former radio disc jockey who emceed several large concerts says: "We once tossed a few dozen Frisbees out to the crowd to keep them busy for a few minutes until the band was ready to take the stage. It worked great...until people figured out they could throw the Frisbees *back*. There's nothing quite as frightening as staring into a spotlight and having five or six Frisbees whiz by your head, thrown from back around row forty-five. One Frisbee slammed into the drum set. The drummer was not pleased."

3. Keep games simple and quick.

As always, you should be able to summarize game rules in a few sentences. But it's especially important to keep rules simple with special-events games. Once these games begin, you generally don't get a chance to clarify or re-explain, so make sure your explanation is foolproof the first time.

4. Make sure everyone gets involved.

It's doubtful that everyone in your group will choose to bob for apples in a toilet. (See page 96.) But everyone can cheer or even dry off the faces of teammates who did. In the same way, it's unlikely that everyone in a crowd of seven hundred will touch the beach balls bouncing around in a game of volleyball. But the possibility *exists*—and that alone can keep a crowd on its feet.

Of course, you should do what you can to increase involvement. If a game calls for five beach balls, use fifteen to increase the odds of everyone getting a chance of hitting a ball. Design games so moving items from one place to another requires them to pass through as many hands as possible. Think of various ways that kids can be involved in the game.

Games planned for special days and special events will pump fun into otherwise predictable meetings and break up the monotony of sometimes boring programs. Use them—but plan ahead so they work to your full advantage and don't just serve as a distraction. As you do, create your own special games or try these field-tested, kid-pleasing games to get you started! One hint: You'll find games for special days in the first half of the chapter and games for special events in the second half.

Affirmation Gifts games for special days
Karen Dockrey

Game Summary: Kids will wish each other "Happy Birthday"—with affirmations.

Game Supplies: You'll need index cards, pencils, crayons or markers, newsprint, birthday cupcakes or cookies, candles, matches, and a hat or box.

The Game:

Birthdays can be sensitive subjects to kids. Some teenagers are younger than everyone thinks, while some are surprisingly older—and not everyone appreciates being in the spotlight when birthday time rolls around.

So celebrate everyone's birthday at once with a party that gives kids the gift of personalized affirmations. To begin, ask everyone to write his or her name and birthday on an index card. When everyone is done, collect the cards in a box or hat.

Then ask kids each to draw a card from the box, returning it and drawing another only if they draw their own name. Set out markers (or crayons) and newsprint. Then have kids form pairs, making sure they are not paired with the person whose name they drew. Tell kids they have five minutes to work with their partners to create brief, *specific* affirmations for the persons whose names they drew. Encourage kids to use the markers to create bold, colorful written or symbolic affirmations.

Explain that affirmations must be positive, encouraging, and true. This isn't the time to be negative, cutting, or sarcastic. Give several examples of affirmations such as "You're such a good singer that you should sing 'Happy Birthday to You' to yourself. No one could do it better" or "You're a good friend who always listens well. Thanks, and happy birthday!"

After five minutes, have kids give the affirmations to the people they were written for. Then lead the group in a rousing rendition of "Happy Birthday to You." Conclude the celebration by serving each person a birthday cupcake or cookie—make sure everyone has a candle to blow out.

While kids enjoy their treats, ask them to discuss how true the affirmations would be if they were shuffled and redistributed. Try to help kids realize that they have each been uniquely created and gifted by God.

Variation idea

If group members know each other well, collect the affirmation cards. Then read them one at a time while kids try to guess who is being described. Then present each card to the person it describes while everyone sings "Happy Birthday to You" to him or her.

If You Love Me, Honey, Smile games for special days
Joanne Knittle

Game Summary: Kids will celebrate Valentine's Day by trying to get each other to smile.

Game Supplies: No supplies are required.

The Game:

Gather kids in a group. Explain that the goal of this game is for kids to get someone of the opposite sex to smile by delivering the line, "If you love me, honey, smile." Although kids can deliver the line any way they wish, they may not touch anyone.

Point out that the best results generally come when the line is delivered with as much drama as possible. Tell your kids to sing it, to beg on their knees, or to impersonate a famous character (perhaps Arnold Schwarzenegger?) delivering the line.

> **★ All-Star ★**
> **anecdote**
>
> Joanne Knittle remarks, "Even the shy kids like this game because they generally don't have the courage to flirt, but in this game, it's OK."

Choose several teenagers to start the game—one for every five kids in your group works well. Direct them to approach kids of the opposite sex and to deliver the line. If the person hearing the line smiles, he or she must deliver it to someone who has not yet been approached or who has not smiled when approached. If the person hearing the line doesn't smile, the person delivering the line must try to get someone else to smile.

Allow kids to play for five minutes or until everyone has had a chance to hear or deliver the line.

Team Time games for special days
Walt Mueller

Game Summary: Kids will play a variety of games with their parents, which is an excellent idea for Mother's Day or Father's Day.

Game Supplies: You'll need supplies for whatever games you decide to play.

The Game:

Parents of teenagers already know their kids often consider them a bit…well, "uncool." And many families don't spend enough quality time together. You can address both problems by inviting parents in for a night of fun games! Some kids may not be able to convince their parents to come. Be sensitive to their situation by having them team up with another family.

Any game will work as long as everyone can play it, the rules are simple, and it's fun. In fact, you might consider organizing a "retro" game night. Ask your group members' parents to drag games they've been saving out of their closets and bring them to your meeting. Try to balance action games such as Twister with calmer games such as Checkers, Charades, or Dominoes and card games such as Hearts, Old Maid, or Go Fish.

For maximum team-building effectiveness, require parents and their kids to be on the same team or to play the same game. Keep the pace moving by having family teams periodically move from game to game.

Conclude the game time by asking parents and teenagers to form small family groups to discuss the following questions:

★ **What did you enjoy about playing as a family? What didn't you enjoy?**

★ **How did playing games together draw you closer together as a family?**

★ **What fun activities could you do every week to draw closer to each other?**

All-Star advice

Bart Campolo observes: "A lot of kids don't come from strong family systems. When I was in youth group, we played Monopoly at home, so playing it at youth group would've been stupid. It wouldn't have been special. But the kids I work with now haven't even played Charades. That's something that families used to do, but many of today's kids probably haven't played Old Maid, Go Fish, or any of those games. We used to bend over backwards to be awesomely creative with games such as Paintball-Superstar-Over the World- Relay. Then we realized we could get away with Tick-Tack-Toe because our kids haven't played Tick-Tack-Toe." There's probably no better time to play these "family games" than on a family game night when kids and parents can play together.

Bob in the Basin games for special days
Jim Burns

Game Summary: Kids will celebrate Halloween or a fall festival by bobbing for apples in a toilet.

Game Supplies: You'll need one absolutely new toilet bowl, apples, towels, and a large cardboard box.

All-Star advice

It's essential you have an absolutely new, unused, never-installed toilet for this game. Of course, you don't necessarily have to share that information with your group. It adds a certain elegance to the game if—as kids participate—you hint broadly that you picked up the toilet at a very reasonable rate when the old city bus station closed. Explaining the toilet's pedigree is up to you.

The Game:

This game will create memories for your kids, especially if you bring a camera and take pictures of the contestants. To prepare for the game, find a new toilet. Toilets are surprisingly inexpensive at builders-supply stores or department stores, or you can borrow a toilet from a local plumber or plumbing-supply store. Make sure that the toilet is completely clean and then seal the trap with duct tape or an easily removed plug—the toilet needs to hold water in the bowl.

Set the toilet in your meeting room before kids arrive. Then cut the bottom out of the cardboard box and set it over the toilet. Make absolutely certain no one knows what's in the box until you're ready to reveal the secret.

When kids arrive, have them form two teams. Explain that teams will compete in a game many of them played as children: Bobbing for Apples. Show the apples you'll be using and assure kids that you have towels for drying their hair.

Explain that, just as in the usual game, kids must grab the apples with their teeth or lips—no hands!—and lift them from the water. In addition, each bobber has thirty seconds to grab an apple. Kids can keep and enjoy any apples they grab. If they don't succeed in thirty seconds, they must step aside and let the next contestant give it a try.

All-Star anecdote

Game contributor Jim Burns reports, "There were a couple of kids who wouldn't play this game, but they laughed like crazy when they watched."

If everyone understands the rules, remove the cardboard box to reveal that kids will be bobbing for apples in a toilet. Pause a few seconds, giving kids a chance to reconsider their decision to play this game. Don't force anyone to participate, but remind kids that their team has a better chance of winning if everyone on the team participates.

Play the game, awarding one hundred points for each apple successfully lifted from the toilet. For extra fun, videotape this event and show the tape later while you serve apples or apple chips as snacks.

Christmas Carol Charades games for special days
Karen Dockrey

Game Summary: Kids will work with teammates to guess the titles of Christmas songs being "drawn."

Game Supplies: You'll need slips of paper, pencils, a paper bag, blank sheets of paper, markers, and a stopwatch.

The Game:

Explain that you're going to play a game of Pencil Charades, which involves drawing symbols on a piece of paper and seeing how long it takes someone to identify the word or phrase being represented.

Give everyone a pencil and several slips of paper. Instruct kids to write the title of one Christmas carol or holiday song on each slip. Encourage kids to write titles of both religious songs and fun seasonal songs. Give anyone who has more ideas than slips as many slips as he or she needs. If someone has a difficult time thinking of songs, let him or her browse through a hymnal or contemporary holiday song-book for ideas.

After several minutes, collect the slips in the paper bag. Then form two teams. If you have more than ten kids in your group, form multiple teams of five or fewer. Explain that you will draw a slip of paper out of the bag and then secretly show one person from each team the title of the Christmas carol you drew. (Don't use any song more than once.) These kids will then each silently draw a picture on the sheet of paper that should enable their teammates to guess the title of the song. The drawers may not use words to convey the title. Everything must be drawn, although

This game is particularly fun when you add nontraditional Christmas or winter songs such as "I Saw Mommy Kissing Santa Claus," "Jingle Bell Rock," "White Christmas," or "We Wish You a Merry Christmas." Kids may or may not know all these songs, so be ready to hum a few bars of each.

letters and numbers may be used as symbols so long as only one is used in each title.

Have teams race to see how fast they can identify each Christmas carol. Teams will receive one point for every second it takes them to identify a song, so each team needs to keep guessing until it gets the right answer. Be sure to record each team's score after every round. Play until everyone has had a chance to draw or until you run out of songs. Reward the winning team—the team with the fewest points—by having everyone else serenade them with four or five Christmas carols. Then distribute candy canes to kids to reward them for their efforts.

Polaroid Scavenger Hunt games for special days
Jim Burns

Game Summary: Kids will have Christmas cheer as they combine a traditional caroling party with a Polaroid scavenger hunt.

Game Supplies: You'll need the following items for every six kids: a Polaroid camera, a pack of film, a watch, a permanent marker, and a photocopy of the "Christmas Wish List" (p. 108).

The Game:

Before the meeting, arrange to have one adult volunteer for every six kids in your group.

To begin, form teams of six. Give each team a Polaroid camera, a pack of film, a watch, a permanent marker, and a photocopy of the "Christmas Wish List" (p. 108). Explain that teams are to go door-to-door singing Christmas carols and taking pictures of the items on the handout. (If kids are uncertain which Christmas carols to sing, spend a few minutes listing all the possibilities.)

Tell teams they are to go to a door and ask if they can take a picture of one or more of the items on the list. If someone agrees to let them take a picture, team members must sing a carol, have the person rate the singing from 1 ("It sounded like cows dying slowly of food poisoning") to 10 ("I thought it was a heavenly choir") and then sign the picture.

Only the adult volunteer may operate the camera, and teams can "collect" no more than two items at any location. Teams have thirty minutes to collect their items and to return to your meeting place—for every minute a team is late, they'll lose the opportunity to present one photo to the group.

After synchronizing watches, send teams out to serenade the neighborhood and scavenge for their items. Then, when teams have returned, ask them to share their pictures and stories!

What's Wrong With This Story? games for special days
Karen Dockrey

Game Summary: Kids will have a fun time discovering what the Bible really says about Christmas.

Game Supplies: You'll need two Bibles.

The Game:

Our culture has so modified and sanitized the Christmas "story" that it's no longer understood as God invading history in the form of a baby being born in an unscrubbed animal pen. Instead, the story has become the heartwarming fable of a tiny baby visited by shepherds, wise men, and probably even Santa. To help your kids discover what really happened two thousand years ago, challenge them to identify what's wrong with the typical Christmas story.

To begin, have kids form two teams. Give each team a Bible. Ask for two volunteers to read aloud Luke 2:1-20 and Matthew 2:1-12. Encourage kids to pay close attention—there will be a quiz later on.

All-Star advice

Instead of having kids raise their hands before answering a question, let the team that sings the phrase "Joy to the world, the Lord has come" most quickly answer first.

After both passages have been read, ask the following questions. (Answers are in parentheses.) Award one thousand points for each correct answer. Ask:

★ **How tall was the wooden stable in which Jesus was born?** (It may have been a cave, not a wooden stable.)

★ **True or false? The census in Judea was initiated by the Romans, not the Jewish leadership.** (True.)

★ **How old was the shepherd boy who visited Jesus?** (No shepherd boy appears in the Bible story.)

★ **True or false? When the angels appeared to the shepherds, there was just one angel visible at first.** (True.)

★ **How high up was the angel who appeared to the shepherds?**
(The Bible actually states that the angel "stood" before them.)

★ **True or false? The star leading the wise men actually moved to lead them to Jesus.** (True.)

★ **Why did the angels state there would be peace among all men?** (They didn't. They said there would be peace to those on whom God's favor rests.)

★ **How many wise men visited Jesus?** (Scripture doesn't say.)

★ **How old was the drummer boy?** (No drummer boy appears in the Bible story.)

★ **True or false? The wise men found the star over the stable.**
(False. In fact, they may have arrived more than a year after Jesus was born. Matthew 2:11 indicates that they entered a house.)

Reward the winning team by having the other team sing several Christmas carols to them.

Group Impressions games for special events
Wayne Rice

Game Summary: Kids will work with team members to pantomime various group activities.

Game Supplies: You'll need a bandanna or a flag, sheets of paper, black markers, and candy.

The Game:

Divide the audience into two teams. Select four or six judges—youth leaders work well—and position them on the stage facing the audience. Give each judge a black marker and as many pieces of paper as you'll have rounds of the game.

Introduce the judges as international experts who will determine scores for the performances they're about to see, much as Olympic judges rate a gymnastic performance as an 8.5 or a 10. The decision of the judges will be final.

Explain that team members are to work together to pantomime a series of actions. When you announce the type of impression teams are to perform, teams will have fifteen seconds to do it. When you drop the bandanna or flag, teams are to stop the impression and quiet down before the bandanna or flag hits the floor.

Judges will assign one score for each impression based on
★ the inventiveness of the impression,
★ the extent of team participation, and
★ how quiet a team is when the bandanna hits the floor.

Assign an equal number of judges to each team and then have teams perform their pantomimes. To keep scoring fair, have judges switch teams after each round. Think up pantomimes you would like kids to perform or use the following ideas:

★ You're sitting in the most boring church service in the history of the world.

★ You're in a movie theater watching the saddest movie you have ever seen.

★ You just woke up, looked in the mirror, and discovered that you were a cockroach.

★ You ate in the school cafeteria, and you're dying of food poisoning.

★ You're attending an art gallery, but you don't understand any of the paintings.

★ You're presenting the keynote speech at the International Mime Convention.

★ You're in the crowd at a (fill in the name of a "head banger" rock group) concert.

★ You're a jockey in the Kentucky Derby, and your mount is about to win the race.

★ It's open microphone night at the Elvis Impersonator Cafe, and you're onstage.

★ You're a six-pack of cola that has been shaken so hard that your tops are popping.

Play as many rounds as you'd like and then total the scores. Announce the winning team, and toss handfuls of candy to the members of the winning team as their prize. Then toss candy to the losing team as a consolation prize.

Add extra meaning to this activity by finishing with the following impression: You are a room full of Christians. Then have kids form pairs and discuss the following questions:
★ **Why did you pick the action you picked?**
★ **What is unique about being a Christian?**

All-Star advice

Judges can build excitement by keeping the score close. In addition, the final calculations are quicker and easier if your judges use just whole- and half-numbers.

Variation idea

Darrell Pearson developed a "pest control" version of this game, challenging kids to impersonate the following bugs:
★ praying mantises
★ cockroaches
★ centipedes
★ army ants
★ butterflies
★ grasshoppers
★ mosquitoes

☆ Pass the Socks games for special events
Thom Schultz

☆ All-Star ☆
advice

If you've asked teenagers attending your event to bring clothing for distribution to a service agency, this is a fun way to collect the clothing. You can even play the game with canned goods—though you'll want to collect canned goods in boxes instead of bags!

Variation idea

Place beanbags at the back of each team, and position wastebaskets ten feet from the kids who will get the beanbags last. Explain that, when beanbags reach the front of the team, the people getting them are to toss them into the "baskets." If they miss, team members are to pass another beanbag along the line so they can take another shot. Declare the first team to score a basket the winner. If you're outside, consider passing water balloons.

Game Summary: Kids will pass articles of clothing in this sanctuary relay.

Game Supplies: You'll need one large box of clothing and one duffel bag for each team.

The Game:

Before the game, gather a box of clothing for each team. Place the same number of garments in each box—and avoid underwear!

Divide the audience into teams of roughly equal size by marking off imaginary lines. Make sure kids know which side of the line they are on. Place a box of clothing at the back left corner of each team's area.

Explain that team members are to pass each item of clothing one at a time across the back row, back the other way across the second to last row, and so on until the clothing arrives at the front of the team, having passed through the hands of every team member. Kids may not touch more than one item at a time, so they should not pass an item until the person next to them has empty hands.

Give a duffel bag to each person who is last in his or her team's line. Explain that, when an item of clothing reaches this person, he or she must stuff it into the duffel bag. Then, when all the clothing is in the bag, the bag must be securely tied, tossed on the floor, and sat on.

Play the game. Declare the team that finishes first the winner.

Roll, Roll, Roll Your Roll games for special events
Joani Schultz

Game Summary: Kids will race to unroll and then roll back up a roll of toilet paper.

Game Supplies: You'll need one roll of toilet paper for each row of teenagers.

The Game:

Urge kids in each row to scoot around so there are no large gaps between them and it will be easy to pass along a valuable item that can't be dropped or broken.

Then give the person on the left end of each row or pew a roll of toilet paper. Explain that teams must unroll the toilet paper as they pass it down the row, making sure not to break the paper. Kids may not toss the roll—they must pass it from one person to the next. In addition, everyone must say his or her full name while passing the roll.

If the toilet paper streamer breaks, team members must send the roll back to the first person in the row and start over. When the roll reaches the end of the row, the last person must stand and hold the toilet paper roll above his or her head—all without tearing the paper.

Play the game until every team has finished unrolling its paper to the end of the row. Then tell kids that you really don't want to waste the toilet paper—that wouldn't show good stewardship—so teams are to race to see which row can roll the paper back up again.

All-Star advice

It's always wise to figure out how many supplies you'll need—and then bring 50 percent more. "I don't know how many times I've been at camps where they run out of water balloons after five minutes," says Steve Fitzhugh. "The water fight was supposed to be the main event of the afternoon, but suddenly it's over—and someone's saying, 'I didn't know we'd need so many balloons.'" Don't skimp on supplies, especially those you can't quickly grab off a shelf. What if kids need to practice the game once before actually playing or if the game goes so well kids demand to play it again? Be ready.

Sanctuary Volleyball games for special events
Thom Schultz

Game Summary: Kids will play a riotous game of volleyball without leaving their seats.

Game Supplies: You'll need rope or yellow "caution" tape, large foam balls or beach balls, damp (but not wet) cotton mop-heads hidden in a garbage bag, and a source of music.

The Game:

Divide the audience into two teams by tossing the rope or "caution" tape down the middle. If you're playing in a sanctuary, use the center aisle as your "net." Explain that the tape or rope is a volleyball net and that the goal of the game is for each side to get as many balls as possible on the other side. Tell kids to play as long as music is playing and to immediately stop play when the music stops.

Explain that kids must remain seated at all times—if a ball is hit out of the playing area, you will return it to play. In addition, a ball must be hit at least twice on a side before it goes back over the net. Finally, kids are not allowed to spike the ball.

Make sure everyone understands the rules and then throw in several balls to start the game. After two minutes, abruptly stop the music. Tell kids that they must be professional volleyball players because they're way too talented for this game to challenge them. So you're going to add a bit of excitement—by introducing additional items to the game.

Reach into the garbage bag, and toss out the mop heads. Then start the game again. When you stop the music, count how many balls and mop heads are in each area and declare a winner. Lead everyone in a round of applause for a game well-played.

☆ All-Star advice ☆

Give this game extra excitement by blasting some Beach Boys music during play. "Wipe Out" by the Surfaris is another excellent choice.

Variation idea

Have kids play "Trash Collector." Give each team a stack of newspapers, and tell them the object is to wad up each page and to throw it over to the other side. When you signal the end of the game, declare the side with the least litter the winner. Recycle the newspapers, of course.

The Wave—And Variations games for special events
Wayne Rice (and others)

Game Summary: Kids will burn off energy by cooperatively creating a variety of "waves."

Game Supplies: No supplies are required.

The Game:

Pioneered and perfected in sports stadiums, the Wave is a simple way to get everyone focused and paying attention.

All the Wave requires is for lines of kids to stand up in unison a half-second after the kids next to them stand, raise their arms over their heads, and then sit back down. Simple. Easy. Think of the Wave as synchronized dance for the rhythm-impaired.

The fun comes with creating variations on the theme and getting the audience involved in performing them. Start your audience with the classic Wave. Keep it going by having it "bounce" back and forth from end to end.

> ### ★ All-Star ★
> ### advice
>
> Don't let them see you sweat. You've never led a game for a group of twelve hundred before. You've never *seen* a crowd of twelve hundred. No problem—if you keep this advice in mind. Show no fear. Lead with confidence or you will never convince a group to try the activity or game.

Then lead kids in the following variations of the Wave:

★ **The Classic With Soundtrack**—Add a vocal element to the classic Wave. Instruct the audience to make a "swoosh" or "whoo" sound as they stand. You'll have to demonstrate.

★ **Front to Back**—Start a Wave at the front of the audience, and let it roll to the back. Consider bouncing the Wave off the back wall and having it roll in reverse back to the front row. Be wary of doing this too many times—you may experience seasickness.

★ **Tidal Wave**—Tell kids they'll begin by impersonating the gentle motion of a calm sea (seated, using small hand-motions, and making a gentle "swoosh" sound) and then progress to a few bigger waves (half-standing, with larger hand-motions, and a making a "splash" sound). Suddenly they'll imitate a tremendous tidal wave (a full-fledged Wave with a deafening "roaaaarrrr!" sound effect).

★ **Surfer Competition**—If you have aisles in your auditorium, divide the audience into teams. Ask one volunteer from each team to "surf" his or her team's Wave. That involves dashing down the aisle as the Wave moves from the back of the room to the front. Surfers should try to keep pace with the Wave and pantomime the body movements of a surfer. Ask youth leaders to be judges and allow three tries per team. Don't try this if there are bleachers or steps involved!

Wedding Fire Drill  games for special events
Darrell Pearson

Game Summary: Kids will evacuate the worship area or auditorium in record time.

Game Supplies: No supplies are required.

The Game:

If you've ever been to a wedding, you know that it takes forever to empty the worship space. Not with the Wedding Fire Drill! This game works best in a traditional worship area—a collection of pews divided by a center aisle with an open area at the front and a lobby—but you can use it in any auditorium with aisles.

You'll clear the worship area the same way formal weddings do—with an usher "releasing" each row after the row in front of it exits. The only difference is that teams will compete to clear their sections as quickly as possible.

Divide the audience into teams, one team per section. Select one usher for each team. Prop open all the doors through which kids will exit. Demonstrate how kids must exit so there's no confusion (and no collisions). Explain that the section that is released, returns, and is seated in precisely the same spots first will be declared the winner. Warn the ushers that you'll penalize their team if they release a row too soon—ten seconds for each infraction.

To begin, place the ushers near the back of the worship area. At your signal, they are to race up the aisle and stand at attention by the first pew, as if they were ushers at a formal wedding. Demonstrate the proper technique.

Explain that no one from the second pew may exit until the usher has stepped forward and nodded at them to move. Kids will exit down the center aisle, cut through the lobby, and return to their seats via the side aisle. Everyone must remain seated after they return. Warn every-

---

★ All-Star ★ anecdote

Game contributor Darrell Pearson loves this game. "With a big audience," he remarks, "I think this is as fun a game as I have ever played."

---

one that pushing and shoving may result in disqualification of the team.

If everyone understands the rules, play the game. If kids have a lot of energy to burn off, play several times. That will help kids sit quietly and attentively during the rest of the meeting.

Christmas Wish List handout

Photograph as many of the items listed below as you can in thirty minutes:

- ❑ a package wrapped in red ribbon
- ❑ an aluminum Christmas tree
- ❑ a yard display featuring Santa and the homeowner hugging Santa
- ❑ a wrapped package that looks like a bike
- ❑ a person drinking eggnog
- ❑ a team member posing with the wise men in a nativity scene
- ❑ someone wearing a Santa Claus hat
- ❑ a member of your group sitting on Santa's lap
- ❑ someone you don't know with a candy cane hung on his or her ear
- ❑ someone your group doesn't know holding a Christmas stocking
- ❑ someone you don't know kissing a team member under mistletoe
- ❑ a child in pajamas decorating a Christmas tree
- ❑ Christmas stockings hung by the chimney with care
- ❑ a reindeer
- ❑ a bathroom that's been decorated for Christmas
- ❑ a stranger performing "The Dance of the Sugarplum Fairies"
- ❑ someone you don't know holding two Christmas cards

All-Star Contributors

Mary Arias, a nine-year youth ministry veteran, currently works with urban Hispanics between the ages of thirteen and twenty-five. An important part of her ministry is organizing service projects in which young people minister to others. Mary enjoyed playing Hide-and-Seek as a child. She liked hiding best, "but I usually got caught *really* fast."

David Bryant has spent eight years in youth ministry thus far, and he hopes to spend many more. His program includes several Bible Clubs at local high schools, a thriving drama team, and a Christian version of Planet Hollywood. Dave's favorite game in elementary school was playing army. He never actually served in the military, though. "I got it out of my system early," he says.

Rick Bundschuh is a veteran youth worker, cartoonist, speaker, and author of numerous youth ministry books. He is currently suffering for the cause of Christ in Hawaii as the pastor of Kauai Christian Fellowship. As a teenager he most enjoyed playing Urban Dye-Wars, a game in which he and his friends would fill squirt guns with water and food coloring and then try to shoot each other.

Jim Burns, Ph.D., is the president of the National Institute of Youth Ministry, a nonprofit organization to help young people and their families make wise decisions and enjoy a vital Christian lifestyle. Jim has penned more than twenty-three resource books for youth, parents, and youth workers. As a child Jim was a baseball fanatic. "My brother played for the Chicago White Sox," he explains, "so I was a baseball kid. I *slept* with a bat and a glove."

Bart Campolo is the founder and president of Kingdom Builders Supply, a missionary organization that partners with inner-city churches to design youth programs. During his high school years, Bart and his friends invented a game based on the movie *Warriors*. "Every winter we played it at least a couple of times," he observes, "all the way through college."

As chairman of the youth ministry department at San Jose Christian College, **Les Christie** teaches a variety of youth-related courses—including one on youth group games. Les, a twenty-nine year youth ministry veteran, is also an author and a national speaker. As a child, he enjoyed dodge ball way *way* more than was probably healthy.

Jill DeCesare has served for five years in children's and youth ministry. "I work with the whole gang—toddler to age eighteen," she explains. Jill's greatest accomplishment in ministry has been "helping my kids get closer to the Lord." Jill attributes her success in kickball (from fourth grade to the present) on her ability as a power player. "I kick for the fences," she says.

Karen Dockrey has worked—and played—with youth for over twenty years. She is the author of twenty-five books for youth and youth workers. As a child, Karen was a dedicated Jacks player. "Even scraping my hands on our rough driveway didn't keep me from playing," she says. And yes, she *could* do "tensies."

Miranda Farrell-Myers is a sixteen-year youth ministry veteran. She calls herself a "youth group planter" because she's helped grow large, effective youth groups in several churches. Miranda loves to spend time one-on-one with group members, sipping Coke and enjoying dessert. As a young child, Miranda used to comb her dolls' hair over and over and over… "until they went bald." Pray for her youth group.

Steve Fitzhugh is the Washington, D.C. director for the Fellowship of Christian Athletes and serves nationally as the executive director of PowerMoves, Inc. An accomplished motivator, poet, and vocal artist, Steve has performed for thousands of youth throughout the continent and around the world. Steve not only enjoyed playing football, he was good at it. He played in the NFL for the Denver Broncos.

Andy Hansen has been in youth ministry for twenty-three years and is currently Director of Conferences for Christ In Youth. This keeps Andy busy; twelve thousand young people attend CIY conferences annually. As a child, Andy enjoyed blasting plastic army men off piles of dirt with a BB gun…which pretty much prepared him for youth ministry.

Rick Houston has been in youth ministry for six years, and his youth group has grown phenomenally during that time! Rick, a graduate student at Claremont School of Theology, likes games *a lot*. His favorite game as a child was playing Hide-and-Seek. His specialty: hiding.

Joanne Knittle, an eight-year youth ministry veteran, is certified in youth ministry studies. Joanne has numerous achievements as a youth worker, including developing a leadership team of high school juniors and seniors who help plan events for the younger kids. Together with her husband, Joanne works with "the best kids in the world." Joanne's favorite games as a child were Mother, May I? and Simon Says. But she admits that they're the only games she can remember playing.

Peter Knudsen has been involved in youth ministry for nine years, and he feels that his greatest achievement is "becoming his kids' friend." At six-feet-eleven-inches, Peter has the distinction of being "the tallest pastor around." He enjoyed playing army when he was young. He and his friends attacked each other with BB guns. "You could only use rifles on one pump, and you had to shoot below the neck...maybe."

Rolland Martinson is the professor of pastoral theology and ministry at Luther Seminary. He's a teacher, pastor, author, and a member of the National Council on Family Relations. Rollie has been involved with youth and youth workers for thirty-five years. As a youngster, Rollie was an avid Fox and Goose player.

Tiger McLuen is the executive director of Youth Leadership's Center for Youth and Family Ministry. He puts his twenty-plus years of youth ministry experience to good use in the classroom, teaching youth ministry at Bethel Seminary and Luther Seminary. Tiger is the author of *Equipped to Serve,* a volunteer youth worker training course. A favorite game from his past: Ultimate Frisbee.

Walt Mueller is the president of the Center for Parent/Youth Understanding, a nonprofit organization that helps churches, schools, and community organizations in their efforts to strengthen families. He has been involved in youth and family ministry for over twenty years and has written extensively on youth culture and family issues. He also has the distinction of having played on what he describes as "the world's worst basketball team." For two straight years, St. Mark's Reformed Episcopal Church was beaten by at *least* eighty points every game.

Rich Mullins hasn't always been a best-selling contemporary Christian singer and musician. He also has hands-on youth experience, having served as youth director for a church in Erlanger, Kentucky. Rich's favorite game growing up was "Switch Sides." (See p. 89.)

G. Keith Olson, Ph.D., established Family Consultation Service, a psychotherapy service center, in 1971. During his college and graduate school years, however, he served as a youth pastor. Dr. Olson, author of three books and host of two videotape series, is a regular speaker at national youth conferences.

Les Parrott III, Ph.D., is a professor of psychology and, with his wife (also Dr. Parrott), co-directs the Center for Relationship Development at Seattle Pacific University. Dr. Parrott has written numerous books, including *Helping the Struggling Adolescent* and *A Counseling Guide.* His favorite junk food is a frappucino.

Darrell Pearson is president of Wild Truth Productions, organizers of high-involvement events for teenagers. He presents the youth event, Wild Truth, in more than one hundred North American and European cities every year. Pearson has written fourteen books for youth leaders and is an accomplished singer and guitar player. Darrell's favorite game as a child was Kick the Can, which he and his friends combined with Hide-and-Seek: "If you were found, you could still win by kicking the can at home base before whoever found you kicked it."

David Rahn is professor of Educational Ministries and co-director of the Link Institute at Huntington College. He has written numerous youth ministry articles and is a frequent speaker at youth seminars and conferences. As a child Dave was a particularly adept Capture the Flag player: "I was good on offense because I was a good 'sneaker.' "

Wayne Rice is co-founder of Youth Specialties, Inc. and Director of Understanding Your Teenager, a seminar program for parents. He has written many quality books and resources for youth ministry. Wayne's favorite game as a young child was playing Marbles. "I was pretty good," he explains, but his parents wouldn't let him play "keepsies." It smacked too much of gambling.

John Sanny spent nine years serving Youth With A Mission and leading games in the Philippines, Thailand, India, Nepal, China, Hong Kong, Guam, Fiji, the Cook Islands, New Zealand, the Amazon, New Guinea, and Australia. A highly ranked tennis player, his favorite games as a child were floor hockey and table tennis.

Joani Schultz, Chief Creative Officer of Group Publishing, Inc., has over twenty years of youth ministry experience. Her favorite game as a child? London Bridge. "I liked being part of the bridge," she explains, "because we got to ask the people we caught questions."

Thom Schultz is founder and CEO of Group Publishing, Inc. He launched Group Magazine during the early '70s because he couldn't find any publications to help him in his own ministry. His favorite game as a nine-year-old was Thumper...and he *still* plays the game.

Susie Shellenberger is the editor of Brio magazine, Focus on the Family's monthly publication for teenage girls. She's written several books for youth and youth workers. As a child, Susie was an avid player of Red Light, Green Light. She's considering organizing a game among her colleagues at Focus on the Family.

Dave Stone has been around youth ministry for thirty-five years, and he still loves kids. He's the author of several youth ministry resources as well as an acclaimed speaker. Lately Dave has been working at establishing churches in Russia through youth ministry. His favorite game growing up? Sandlot football: "I was either end or quarterback."

Michael D. Warden has worked in youth ministry for fifteen years and has been involved in creating and writing several resources for youth workers. During his younger days, Michael enjoyed playing "If You Love Me, Honey, Smile." (See p. 94). Michael explains, "I could get *anybody* to smile."